The Ultimate

C2C

Coast to

C000256704

EXCELLENT BOOKS
01924 609148
www.excellentbooks.co.uk
Third edition, 2nd print 2017

Text © Richard Peace 2017
Photographs and illustrations © Richard Peace unless otherwise indicated
Profiles design: Vincent Burgeon
Map bases © OpenStreetMap contributors opendatacommons.org
Cartography © Excellent Books All rights reserved
Overview map pgs 4&5, base mapping © Collins Bartholomew Ltd 2017

Whilst the author has researched the route for the purposes of this guide,
no responsibility can be accepted for any unforeseen circumstances
encountered whilst following it. The publisher would, however, welcome any
information regarding any material changes and any problems encountered.

Front cover photo: Climbing Hartside
Rear cover photo: The coast at Tynemouth, the C2C northern finish option
Frontispiece: The C2C start in Whitehaven

CONTENTS

ROUTE TOTALS
WHITEHAVEN - SUNDERLAND OPTION 215 km 133 miles
WORKINGTON - SUNDERLAND OPTION 202 km 125 miles
WHITEHAVEN - TYNEMOUTH OPTION 222 km 137.5 miles
WORKINGTON - TYNEMOUTH OPTION 209 km 129.5 miles

Look out for National Cycle
Network mileposts along the way.
This one is at North Shields .

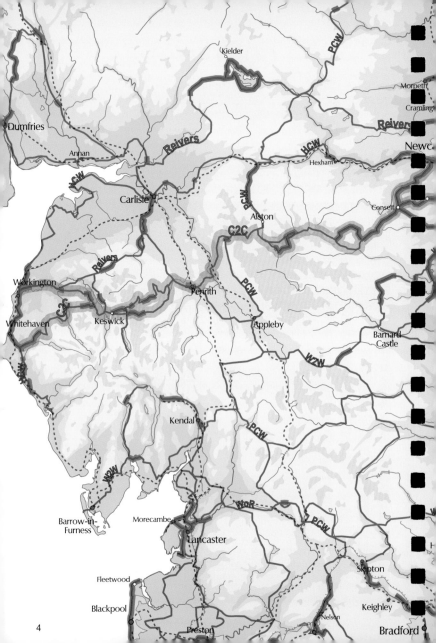

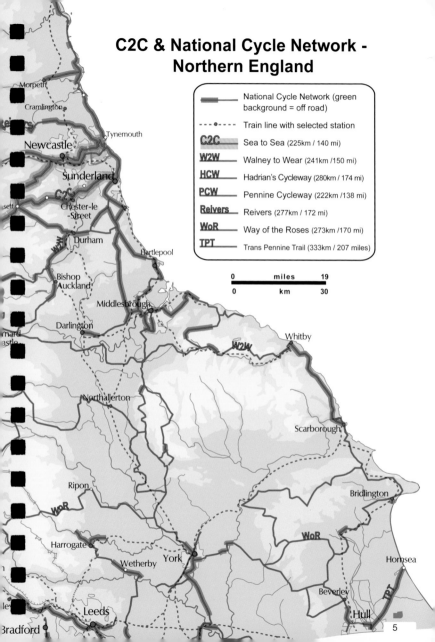

C2C & National Cycle Network - Northern England

	National Cycle Network (green background = off road)
- - -•- - -	Train line with selected station
C2C	Sea to Sea (225km / 140 mi)
W2W	Walney to Wear (241km /150 mi)
HCW	Hadrian's Cycleway (280km /174 mi)
PCW	Pennine Cycleway (222km /138 mi)
Reivers	Reivers (277km / 172 mi)
WoR	Way of the Roses (273km /170 mi)
TPT	Trans Pennine Trail (333km / 207 miles)

0	miles	19
0	km	30

5

The C2C - Coast to Coast by Bike

The route

The C2C can fairly claim to be the most popular and most widely known long distance cycle route in the UK, completed by many thousands of people each year. The longest option runs for nearly 140 miles over the northern edge of the Lake District, across the Eden Valley and across the beautifully bleak Northern Pennines before dropping down to the post-industrial landscape of the North-East. There are optional starting points (Whitehaven or Workington) and a choice of end point (Tynemouth or Sunderland).

The route uses a mix of specially constructed cycle paths, off-road tracks and minor roads, only very occasionally straying onto short sections of busier road where necessary.

Well signed along its length, it can be completed by the whole gamut of cyclists, whilst not being designed for any specific sub-group of the cycling world, such as mountain-bikers or tourers. Although undoubtedly a challenge, containing several serious climbs, it is completed by those with little experience of cycling and committed bikers alike. Careful choice of alternative sections should allow just about any type of bike to complete the route (tricycles and bike trailers may have difficulty passing around barriers and on some climbs). However, having a wide range of gears will be a godsend and avoid much uphill pushing.

Many of the minor roads used by the C2C are idyllically quiet such as this one near Thackthwaite on the Old Coach Road option

Why so popular? The C2C was the brainchild of Sustrans, the UK's leading sustainable transport charity, which has promoted the C2C as a 'flagship' long-distance route and it has undoubtedly tapped a demand for long-distance cycle holidays. Some first-rate support facilities have developed around the route. Underlying all this is the desire to escape the traffic on two wheels, surely a reaction against the road congestion that has become one of the great logistical and health problems of our age. Many previous non-cyclists have successfully attempted this challenging route and have become more regular cyclists. The C2C has also become extremely popular with charity rides and has certainly played its part in raising huge sums for a wide range of charities.

Approaching the Lake District proper east of Kirkland

The C2C takes in fantastic scenery. The mountains of the Lake District yield to the subtler but equally beautiful Eden Valley, around Penrith. A very stiff climb up Hartside onto the rolling Pennines provides a further contrast. Settlements are relatively few hereabouts and winter weather can be the most extreme on the whole route. Former lead mining settlements such as Allenheads provide opportunities for sleep and refreshment whilst the landscape also bears reminders of the defunct lead mining industry in the form of old shafts, flues and numerous other constructions. Although the North-East is often associated with the unemployment caused as a result of heavy industrial decline, it has splendid visitor attractions and remarkable architecture, for example in Newcastle city centre.

The Wearmouth and Tyne bridges, in Sunderland and Newcastle respectively, and the Gateshead Millennium Bridge, are fittingly dramatic heralds to the two finishing points. It's hardly surprising, then, that after negotiating two of the country's main mountain ranges and at least one major city, and linking the Irish and North Seas in the process, a real sense of achievement in completing this epic journey is just about inevitable!

Sustrans and the National Cycle Network

Sustrans is a leading UK charity enabling people to travel by foot, bike or public transport for more of the journeys they make everyday. Sustrans is behind many groundbreaking projects, including the National Cycle Network, over 14,000 miles of signed cycling and walking routes on traffic-free paths and quiet roads across the UK.

Created from one of the first ever National Lottery grants in 1995, the popularity of the Network has grown enormously and it now carries over a million walking and cycling journeys daily and passes within a mile of 57% of the population.

The maintenance and the development of the National Cycle Network and Sustrans' other projects rely on the kind donations of Sustrans supporters. **Make your move and support Sustrans today!** Visit www.sustrans.org.uk or call 0300 3032604 to find out more.

Route surface and signage

The C2C typifies the qualities of the NCN; high quality cycling and walking routes criss-crossing the country that even extend across major urban centres (Sunderland and Newcastle in the case of the C2C).

Many of the traffic-free paths are tarmac and even where they are not the surface is usually compact, well-drained and free-rolling (the occasional rough sections are indicated with an exclamation mark sign on the maps). The NCN's blue, white and red signage soon becomes familiar as you cycle along. As well as very prominent direction signing at junctions also look out for the red and white route number patches and smaller signs that are found stuck at the side of the road, reassuring confirmations you are still on the route. Currently around 45% of the route is traffic-free (the exact % depends on route option).

Signed and mapped, all major routes on the NCN are identified by route number and those used by the C2C are summarised below:

Route	From	To
NCN 71	Whitehaven or Workington	Blencow near Penrith
NCN 7	Blencow near Penrith	Sunderland
NCN 1	Sunderland	Roker
NCN 14	Consett	River Tyne and Tyne Tunnel (Keelman's Way option)
NCN 72	River Tyne	North Shields
NCN 1	North Shields	Tynemouth

Other popular NCN routes either cross or coincide with the C2C, namely Hadrian's Cycleway (NCN 72), the Reivers (NCN 10) and the Pennine Cycleway (NCN 68). These are clearly signed and should not be confused with the C2C or followed instead of it. Where the C2C occasionally shares a section of one of these routes, for example with the Pennine Cycleway up Hartside and to Alston it is made clear you are also following the C2C and when NCN 68 separates in Alston, signing again should be obvious.

Route options are well signed

How long should I take?

How long you allow yourself depends on experience, fitness and choice of route. Although some ultra-fit enthusiasts aim to do the whole route in less than 24 hours, the vast majority of C2Cers are holidaying and usually take between three and seven days. Some keen cyclists, especially those with previous experience of the route, complete it over a long weekend. Most people seem to go for three days to complete the route in reasonable comfort but without too much in the way of sightseeing or diversions. For a more leisurely experience allow four days or more.

This guide is split into five 'day' sections, ranging from to 36 to 52km (22 to 32 miles), aimed at novice cyclists or those with plenty of time who want to take in some attractions, with section start and finish points at or near major population centres to ensure plenty of accommodation and other services. For two-day trips Garrigill or Alston make good overnight stops if you're doing well, or even Nenthead if you're really moving. They're just beyond the half way stage and have a good amount of accommodation - this will give you a much easier second day. Only recommended for very fit cyclists who enjoy the major challenge of covering around 70 miles on each of two consecutive days over some very hilly terrain.

Sporty cyclists at Whitehaven

For three-dayers there are plenty of places to stay in and between Keswick and Penrith for night one. Places between Allenheads and Castleside all have accommodation for night two but as the second half of the route is easier, it may not stop you finishing the journey as planned if your second night is around Nenthead. Still a stiff challenge for sporty and fit cyclists. Four-day trips and beyond introduce countless permutations of how the journey can be split up. A not too recent survey suggested that overall Keswick and Nenthead were the most popular overnight halts.

With the right preparation and conditions, the C2C can be whatever sort of route you want to make it - a strenuous challenge route through to a leisurely recreational route. Do have a realistic idea of what daily mileage you are comfortable achieving; remember that the C2C has a large range of terrain and difficulty, from the considerable challenge of the Old Coach Road alternative to flat cyclepaths, so adjust time estimates accordingly. The route descriptions and profiles at the beginning of each section of this book give a good idea of what to expect.

When should I go?

The route is designed to be useable all year round although a winter trip will need more care and planning and may not be advisable if the weather does not promise well. Potentially extreme weather conditions mean you should be particularly wary of crossing the Penrith to Nenthead section between November and April. Weather forecasts should be taken into account whatever the time of year. Good detailed forecasts can be had at www.metoffice.gov.uk and www.bbc.co.uk/weather. All these will provide temperature, wind direction, visibility, outlook and more. George Fisher - www.georgefisher.co.uk - the outdoor store in Keswick has a live webcam view of conditions in Keswick.

It is advisable to book accommodation as far in advance as practicable, especially in summer or if you are planning to stay in smaller settlements with only limited accommodation. Some accommodation providers,usually in the very busy spots such as Keswick, or at very busy times such as bank holidays may have minimum stay requirements of more than one night. Those wanting to camp along the way should certainly have some previous cycling experience and allow extra time as the extra weight slows down even the fittest cyclist quite noticeably.

Whatever time of year you're going, be prepared - typically, it rains on about one day in three in England, probably more in The Lake District and Pennines. The higher you go, the more likely it is to be cold and windy and there's always the possibility of hill fog. Poor weather is one of the things most often cited in a 2000 survey as most detracting from enjoyment of the route. If you are in a position to plan very short-term, it may well help.

It can be sunny in the Lakeland valleys and thick cloud above

Supported or unsupported?

If you opt to travel unsupported (i.e carry your own luggage) this need not necessarily mean carrying too much extra weight as everything from spare clothing to bike accessories has got lighter over the years. Carrying full camping gear will inevitably add weight you will notice though, especially going up steep hills.

If you want the convenience and comfort of motorised luggage transfer, having all your accommodation arranged for you and having an emergency backup service at the end of a phone line, there is a number of companies that offer combinations of various services including motorised back-up, accommodation booking and luggage transfer. Here is a quick summary:

Company	Contact	Services
Adventure Cycling	0773 6816700 www.adventurecycling.co.uk	Fully guided bespoke rides. Qualified instructors. Penrith based.
The Bike Bus	01207 237424 www.stanley-travel.com	Self-guided. Stanley based.
C2C Hassle Free	01768 898342 www.c2chasslefree.co.uk	Self-guided. From Mains Farm bunkhouse, Kirkoswald (pgs 70-71).
Cycle Active	01768 840400 cycleactive.com	Self-guided. Alternative mountain bike options available.
Ecocabs	01434 600600 www.600600.co.uk/bike-transport	Biodiesel taxi service based in Hexham offering bike and luggage transport.
Haven Cycles	01946 63263 www.havencycles-c2cservices.co.uk	Services include insured car parking, rescue and baggage transfer. Whitehaven based.
Macs Adventure	0141 530 5259 www.macsadventure.com	Self-guided & group option. 15kg baggage limit. Bike hire available.
Mickledore	017687 72335 www.mickledore.co.uk	Self-guided with baggage transfer option
Norcroft	01768 862365 www.norcroft-guesthouse.co.uk	Bike / e-bike hire and luggage transport, return to route start etc
Pedal Power	01665 713 448 www.pedal-power.co.uk	Self-guided with back up services including bike hire.
Saddle Skedaddle	0191 2651110 www.skedaddle.co.uk	Options include full backup from support van which is on hand throughout.
Sherpa Van	www.sherpavan.com 01748 826917	Door to door baggage moving. From £7 per bag per day.
Trailbrakes	07922 653327 www.trailbrakes.co.uk	Self-guided tours with bunkhouse options.
Xplore	www.xplorebritain.com 01325 313609	Self-guided tours based in County Durham.

Riding Information & Advice

Preparing for the ride
Before you go check your bike is in good condition with tyres pumped up and seat and handlebars set to the right position. Check brakes and lights are in good order and tightly secured, gears are changing smoothly, and gear and brake cables aren't rusty or frayed. Wheel quick releases should be in the closed position and the chain should be clean and lubricated.

What to wear
You shouldn't need to invest in lots of specialist clothing or footwear to enjoy the C2C. Wear thin layers which you can easily add or remove as you go, and choose light, breathable fabrics, though be aware when you are comfortably warm at low altitudes some extra insulation may be needed on the summits, even on warm summer days. Take a waterproof, hat and gloves (your extremities are more exposed when cycling), and if you're going to be cycling at night, take a bright, reflective top (not a bad idea in the daytime either). Padded shorts can be helpful for extra comfort when riding too.

Useful kit list
- Puncture repair kit & pump
- Tyre levers & spare inner tubes
- Water bottle
- Bike oil or lubricant
- Bike lights
- Bike 'multi-tool' or Allen keys & adjustable spanner
- Bike lock, bungee cords & panniers to carry luggage

Bike accessories
A bike bell is a must as it lets you warn pedestrians of your approach. Helmets are not compulsory so the decision is a question of individual choice – however although helmets can't prevent accidents they can protect you if they do occur and are especially recommended for young children.

Prepare well and have trouble-free fun

Easy cycling on the railpath out of Whitehaven

Cycling with children

The C2C is generally easygoing at either end, well-suited to children, but tough in the middle where older children with good climbing ability will feel more at home than the very young cyclist.

If cycling with a family, remember to keep children in front of you on roads (or in between if there are two of you), and take special care at road junctions. Plan day stages carefully with plenty of refreshment stops, and remember to keep toddlers wrapped up so they don't lose heat when you're pedalling.

What kind of bike?

The best bike to tackle the C2C on is probably a hybrid bike, rather than a racer, due to the small sections with a rough surface. A wide gear range will be helpful too. However you can use just about any bike if you have experience riding it in all conditions. Small-wheeled Brompton folding bikes and electric bikes have both been used to complete the route.

Good cycling code

- Always follow the Highway Code
- Cycle at a safe and responsible speed
- Give way to pedestrians
- Remember that some people are hard of hearing and visually impaired. Don't assume they can see or hear you
- Where there are wheelchair users or horse riders please give way
- Ring a bell or call out to warn of your approach – acknowledge people who give way to you
- Follow the Countryside Code; in particular respect crops, livestock and wildlife and take litter home
- Take special care at junctions, when cycling downhill and on loose surfaces
- Always carry food, water, a puncture repair kit, a map and waterproofs
- Keep your bike roadworthy; use lights in poor visibility
- Consider wearing a helmet and high visibility clothing

Travel Information

The route is designed to be tackled west to east to take advantage of the prevailing wind which means Whitehaven or Workington is the start point for the vast majority who complete the C2C.

There are several return NCN cycle route options listed on the map at the start of the introduction. However, many C2Cers leave their motor transport at the western end and either use one of the transport / holiday companies listed on page 12 or choose the train return.

Bikes on UK trains

Bikes are carried free of charge on most UK trains, but spaces are usually limited and reservations sometimes required, especially on intercity services. Reserve a space for your bike when you book or by calling the train operator. For rail access see the NCN Northern England map at the beginning of the guide. The bike booking system for rail services can be complex. At the time of press the system was as follows:

To take a bike on intercity services advance seat reservations (normally no extra charge) are all but essential.

Local services around the C2C are likely to be run by either Northern or possibly Scotrail. Northern allocate bike space on a first-come, first-served basis. Neither company charges but Scotrail may require a free reservation on some long distance services.

Once you know your travel times it is advisable to check with the relevant train company websites at **www.nationalrail.co.uk** where you can also check times and book tickets (03457 484950 for National Rail enquiries). **Note:** Each chapter has more detailed information about train companies serving stations on or near that route section.

A useful leaflet is **"Cycling by train"** produced by Brompton and available at railway stations or downloadable from www.nationalrail.co.uk. It gives the cycle carriage rules position of each company and phone number. See also **www.atob.org.uk**

Northern Rail services are 'roll-on roll-off', subject to space

Trains from Tynemouth to Newcastle are part of the Newcastle Metro system and do not take bikes other than folders, so you may have to retrace your tracks back to Newcastle Central station. If heading back to Whitehaven from Sunderland you'll have to cycle or get the train back to Newcastle.

Accommodation listings and contacts

The listings in the guide shown with blue numbering have been chosen because they are near the route. They are of course just a cross-section of what is available and by travelling a little further off the route plenty more accommodation opportunities open up.

Important note: In 'tourist honeypot' areas (in and around Keswick in particular) it may be difficult to book for a single night in high season or weekends, owners often preferring a minimum of two nights. We have tried to highlight which establishments do this in the text but be aware it can be a potential difficulty and establishments can change their policy so booking ahead will pay off in these areas.

There are several national organisations that also offer accommodation or listings services that might prove useful:

Beds for Cyclists **www.bedsforcyclists.co.uk**
Camping and Caravanning Club **www.campingandcaravanningclub.co.uk**
Visit Britain **www.visitbritain.com**
Youth Hostels Association **www.yha.org.uk**
Independent Hostel Guide **www.independenthostelguide.co.uk**
There are also a couple of C2C specific listings sites:
www.c2c-guide.co.uk
www.c2cplaces2stay.co.uk

C2C survey findings and other facts

- 69 % of users surveyed were travelling east.
- Most got to the route by bike - only 8% came in a car.
- All were there for leisure purposes - 44% as part of a holiday.
- Average age was 38.   • 85% were male.
- The average amount of cycling in a day was 6.1 hours.
- The majority of users were regular, experienced cyclists but 25% were occasional cyclists including a few new to the activity.
- A 4 year old has completed the C2C in 3 days. He pedalled a 'tagalong' bike attached to his dad's cycle. It was completed for fun and as a fund raiser for a cancer charity; the little boy's mother died from the disease.
- Doing the C2C in a day is a challenge for only the fittest and most serious of cyclists. The quickest time we have heard of is around 12 hours - an average of around 11 miles per hour cycling continuously or 12 miles per hour with an hour's food break.
- The C2C has been completed by Brompton folding bike but perhaps the craziest group of all completed the route on large-wheeled unicycles!

Cooling off in summer on the Old Coach Road option east of Keswick

Kirkland village has an
impressive backdrop

Whitehaven ~ Keswick

You are soon on cycle path after leaving Whitehaven's centrepiece, its regenerated harbour, passing by several former iron mining villages. The true mountains of the Lake District are soon in sight, heralded by pleasant villages such as Loweswater and High Lorton (the former little more than a church and a beautiful Lakeland inn) as you dip and climb on quiet minor roads.

After Kirkland and Lamplugh there are spectacular views down to Ennerdale Water and back over the coastline then a lovely section alongside the quiet depths of Loweswater before the steep but spectacular climb over the Whinlatter Pass. Dropping down, the quaint villages of Braithwaite and Portinscale are linked by glorious little roads along the Newlands Valley to one of the epicentres of Lakeland tourism, Keswick.

Route Info

Distance 52 km (32 miles)

Off - road 19 km (12 miles) The railpath out of Whitehaven is generally nice quality tarmac, apart from the last small section around Rowrah which is reasonable quality crushed stone. The tracks at Whinlatter are broad, reasonably-surfaced forest tracks.

Terrain It's a steady though very gradual climb from Whitehaven up the railpath, exiting after around 16 km (10 miles) onto undulating minor roads with relatively small but testing climbs after Kirkland and Lamplugh. The real test of the day comes crossing the Whinlatter Pass, a lengthy and sometimes steep climb alternating between minor road, forest track and B-road. Blissfully quiet roads approach Keswick but be aware there is a brief main road section approaching Keswick centre that can get busy with motor traffic.

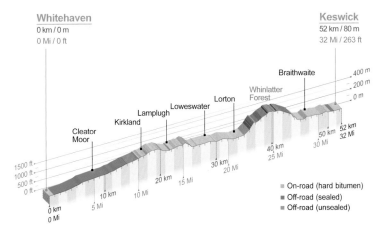

Whitehaven
0 km / 0 m
0 Mi / 0 ft

Keswick
52 km / 80 m
32 Mi / 263 ft

On-road (hard bitumen)
Off-road (sealed)
Off-road (unsealed)

19

What to See & Do

• **Whitehaven** is a listed 'Gem Town' and is the most complete example of planned Georgian architecture in Europe, with many fine individual buildings on Roper Street and Lowther Street and an unusual gridiron street pattern.

The interesting harbour area is a great setting for a sea to sea send off too, with refurbished moorings housing impressive boats, many new sculptures and new lighting backed by some attractive bars and cafes. The sunset can be spectacular here, hitting the harbour walls and buildings and illuminating the sea and the Scottish hills in the distance. The nearby mine remains of Wellington and Duke Pits at South Beach Recreation Area are an interesting short walk away. There's a Candlestick Chimney viewpoint, part of the former Wellington pit (operating 1840-1932) which was the scene of a 1910 mine disaster with 136 lives lost.

The **Beacon Museum** shows the town's connection with slavery, smuggling, mining, shipbuilding and America. St. James' Church has a fine Georgian interior whilst St. Nicholas' Church on Lowther St. is a church tower backed by some fine gardens.

The **Haig Colliery Mining Museum** is situated high on the cliffs above Whitehaven. Closed from summer 2013 for a period of restoration following a lottery grant of over £2 million. **Rum Story** on Lowther Street has lots of interactive exhibits about the town's trade and sells rum.

• **Cleator Moor** has a modern miners memorial sculpture in the market square as well as the Stirling Memorial to a former mine owner. Cleator Moor was known as Little Ireland because of the many Irish immigrants who settled here after the 19th century Irish potato famine. Iron ore mining was the main industry and the cycle path you have come here on once took thousands of tons of ore to Whitehaven harbour.

Whitehaven's attractive harbour at sunset

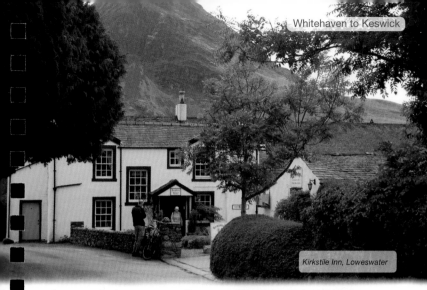

Kirkstile Inn, Loweswater

• **Loweswater** is a gorgeous village of scattered houses and farms, lying between the smallest of the Lakes, Loweswater and Crummock Water, in a spectacular location. The Kirkstile Inn, backed by the peak of Melbreck, and the church, opposite, form the tiny village heart. Large agricultural show every September.

• **Low and High Lorton** are picturesque villages marking the start of your ascent into the Lake District proper. Situated in the flat green Vale of Lorton and surrounded by Lakeland peaks. Lorton Hall has a fifteenth century pele tower and George Fox, the founder of the English Quaker movement, preached behind High Lorton village hall; nowadays it's a beautiful picnic spot by a little beck with the famous Lorton Yew opposite, said to be more than 1000 years old which had a perimeter of nearly 300 feet before it was reduced in size by the ravages of time.

• **Whinlatter Forest & Visitor Centre** is run by the Forestry Commission and open 7 days a week. The **exhibition centre** has good displays for all ages. Two mountain bike trails in the Forest, a 19km red grade and a 7.5km blue grade. Bike hire at Cyclewise shop. **Go Ape** is a treetop adventure assault course.

For Braithwaite, Portinscale and Keswick entries see Keswick to Penrith chapter, pg 47.

Directions

1 This initial section is well signed as NCN route 71. Start by the slipway of the inner harbour by the C2C sculpture. It is traditional to dip your wheel in the sea! Head right then left up Quay St. Go right onto Swingpump Lane and across the mini-roundabout at its end onto New Town, then over another mini-roundabout by Haven Cycles onto Preston Street and very shortly turn left onto a tarmac path. Beware of staggered junction of path shortly as it crosses a road (Coach Road).

Accommodation

❶ THE TIVOLI GUEST HOUSE
156 Queen Street CA28 7BA
01946 67400   www.tivoliguesthouse.co.uk

❷ READ GUEST HOUSE
Cross Street CA28 7BX
01946 61515   www.whitehaven.org.uk/read.html

❸ THE WAVERLEY HOTEL
13-14 Tangier Street CA28 7UX
01946 694337   www.thewaverleyhotel.co.uk

❹ GLENFIELD HOUSE
Back Corkickle CA28 7TS
01946 691911   glenfieldhousewhitehaven.co.uk

Railpath junctions out of Whitehaven are well-signed

If arriving by bike you will be using **Northern** for at least the last part of the journey, possibly a lot more if arriving from elsewhere in Northern England. Their quoted policy is 'Bikes are carried free of charge at any time and you don't need to make reservations. The cycle space on trains is clearly marked, both internally and externally. Space is allocated on a first come, first served basis. We can only carry a maximum of two bikes per train but conductors have responsibility for the safety of their train and have the right to refuse entry if the train is busy.' Tandems and other 'non-standard' bikes are likely to be excluded.
Virgin run lots of trains along the West Coast main line running through Carlisle. Bikes are carried free but an advance reservation is needed and you are supplied with a printed label. Ask a station employee in advance where your allotted space is on the train (you'll only have a few minutes to get your bike and gear aboard). TransPennine Express also use the East Coast main line and carry bikes free with reservations being made at least 24 hours in advance by calling 0345 600 1671 (option 4).

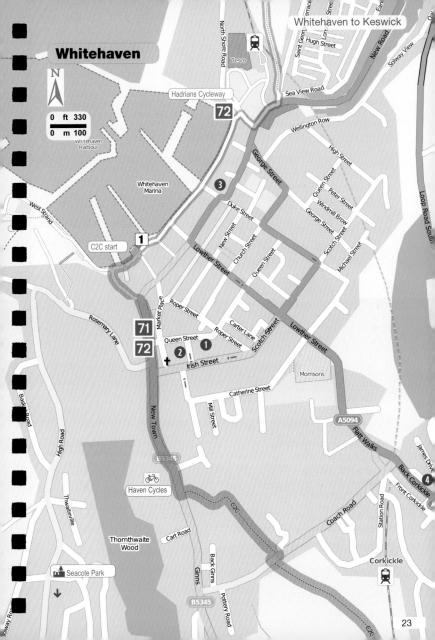

Whitehaven

N

0 ft 330
0 m 100

Hadrians Cycleway

72

Tesco

North Shore Road

New Road

Solway View

Saint George's Terrace

Hugh Street

Long Terrace

Earl Street

Sea View Road

Wellington Row

Whitehaven Harbour

George Street

High Street

Whitehaven Marina

3

Queen Street

Peter Street

Windmill Brow

Duke Street

George Street

Scotch Street

Michael Street

Loop Road South

New Street

Church Street

Queen Street

1

West Strand

C2C start

1

Lowther Street

Market Place

Roper Street

Carter Lane

Scotch Street

Lowther Street

Rosemary Lane

71

72

Queen Street

Roper Street

1

2

Irish Street

Morrisons

Catherine Street

Basket Road

High Road

New Town

Mill Street

A5094

Fatt Walks

Back Corkickle

James Drive

4

Front Corkickle

B5345

Haven Cycles

Station Road

Thwaiteville

C2C

Coach Road

Thornthwaite Wood

Cart Road

Back Ginns

Corkickle

Seacote Park

Ginns

Pottery Road

B5345

C2C

Solway Road

23

2 Under the railway go up the zigzag path and right onto Esk Avenue and then rejoin the path by going right just before an infant's school.

3 Briefly exit the path onto Croasdale Avenue then Wasdale Avenue (route well-signed here at time of writing). Rejoin path to head out of the town.

A handy feature along the traffic-free trail is the cast iron posts showing destinations. Note Hadrian's Cycleway (NCN72) splits off right nearly 7km (4 miles) after your start - you keep to the left here on NCN71. There are a series of seats-cum-sculptures along the way and the fine Phoenix Bridge that you pass under at Cleator Moor (whose town centre is accessible by heading up to the bridge and right).

Look out for the Phoenix Bridge over the trail at Cleator Moor

5 GLENARD GUEST HOUSE
Inkerman Terrace CA28 7TY
01946 692249 www.glenard.co.uk

6 CHASE HOTEL
Inkerman Terrace CA28 8AA
01946 693656
www.chasewhitehaven.co.uk

7 LOWTHER HOUSE
13 Inkerman Terrace CA28 7TY
01946 63169 lowtherhouse-whitehaven.com

8 SUMMERGROVE HALLS
Hensingham CA28 8XZ
01946 813328 summergrovehalls.co.uk
Plenty of rooms for large groups and self-catering option

SEACOTE PARK
The Beach St Bees CA27 0ET,
01946 822 777
www.seacote.com

i **Whinlatter Visitor Centre**
Whinlatter Forest Park
017687 78469
www.forestry.gov.uk/whinlatter

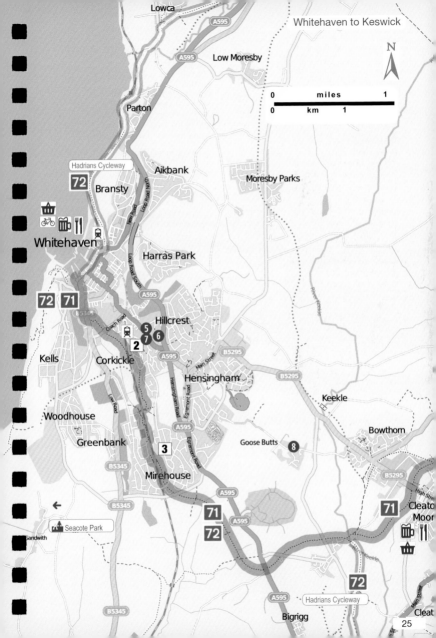

Lowca

A595

Low Moresby

A595

Parton

Moresby Parks

Aikbank

Hadrians Cycleway
72 Bransty

Whitehaven

Harras Park

River Keekle

A595

72 71

Hillcrest
5
2 7 6

Kells

Corckickle

A595

B5295

Hensingham

B5295

Keekle

Coach Road

Loop Road South

Loop Road North

New Road

Main Street

Hensingham Road

Egremont Road

Bowthorn

Woodhouse

Greenbank

3

Mirehouse

Goose Butts
8

B5295

B5345

High Stre...

71 Cleato Moor

Seacote Park

B5345

Egremont Road

71
72 A595

Sandwith

Bigrigg

A595 Hadrians Cycleway

Cleat

9 THE PARKSIDE HOTEL
Parkside Road, Cleator Moor CA25 5HF
01946 811001
www.theparksidehotel.co.uk

10 THE STORK HOTEL
Rowrah Road Rowrah CA26 3XJ
01946 861213 www.storkhotel.co.uk

11 ROWRAH HALL
Rowrah CA26 3XH
01946 861949 / 07775 788680
www.rowrah-hall.co.uk

12 GRANGE COUNTRY HOUSE HOTEL
Loweswater CA13 0SU
01946 861211 / 01946 861570
www.thegrange-loweswater.co.uk

13 ASKHILL FARM
Loweswater CA13 0SU
01946 861640 www.loweswatercam.co.uk

B FELLDYKE BUNKHOUSE
Felldyke Lamplugh CA14 4SH
01900 826698 or 07884 476708
www.felldyke-bunkhouse.co.uk
Groups only - see website for conditions

INGLENOOK CARAVAN PARK
Lamplugh CA14 4SH
01946 861240   Shop on site

B SWALLOW BARN
Waterend Farm Loweswater CA13 0SU
01946 861465 or 01946 758198
www.lakelandcampingbarns.co.uk

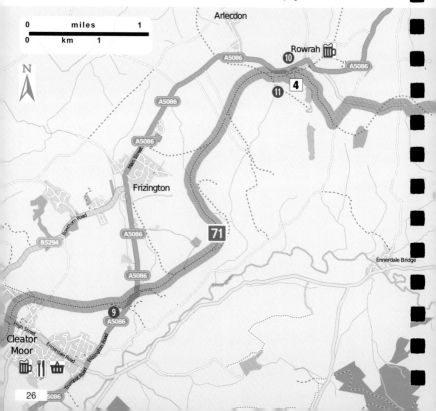

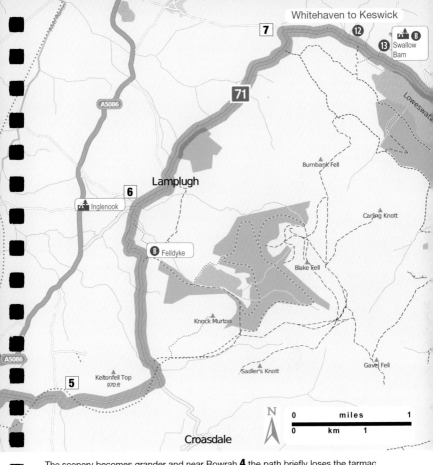

The scenery becomes grander and near Rowrah **4** the path briefly loses the tarmac surface before it ends. Turn left onto the road and at the first T-junction turn right to climb past the school. The small village of Kirkland **5** comes into view with a spectacular Lakeland backdrop and you follow the road into the village. Here head straight across the crossroads and dip and climb through open country, with great views of Ennerdale Water down to the right. Climb to a T-junction and left, the road now levelling out across Knock Fell before dipping and twisting. Keep bearing right at any minor junctions to come into Lamplugh Cross by Inglenook Caravan Park.

6 At the next T-junction head right for Loweswater and Buttermere. Climb and pass the church then take a right signed Loweswater. Follow this long largely level road which has great views back to the coast for around 2.7km (1.7 miles) before hairpinning right **7** to drop down to Loweswater alongside the lake.

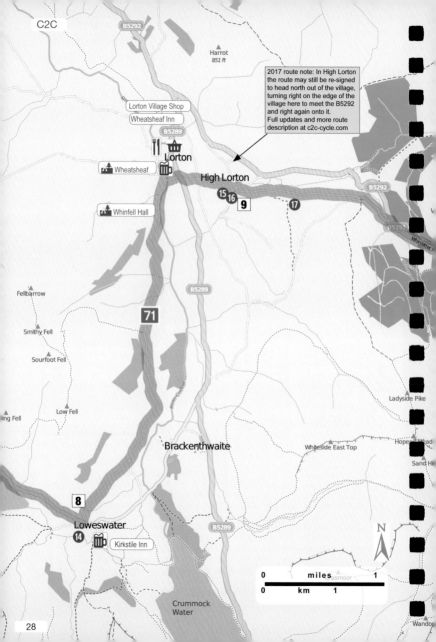

C2C

B5292

Harrot
851 ft

2017 route note: In High Lorton
the route may still be re-signed
to head north out of the
village, turning right on the edge of the
village here to meet the B5292
and right again onto it.
Full updates and more route
description at c2c-cycle.com

Lorton Village Shop
Wheatsheaf Inn

B5289

Lorton

Wheatsheaf

High Lorton

B5292

Whinfell Hall

15 16

9

17

B5292

Whinlatter

Fellbarrow

B5289

71

Smithy Fell

Sourfoot Fell

Ladyside Pike

Low Fell

ng Fell

River Cocker

Brackenthwaite

Whiteside East Top

Hopebeck

Sand Hi

8

B5289

Loweswater

14

Kirkstile Inn

N

0   miles   1
0   km   1

asmoor

Crummock
Water

Wandor

8 About 1km (0.6 miles) after leaving the lakeside at Loweswater turn left, signed Thackthwaite. and follow the lovely tiny road for around 5km (3 miles) to come into Low Lorton. Here turn right at the T-junction to cross the lovely little bridge then bear right then left at the staggered crossroads over the B5289.

9 Bend left into High Lorton and soon turn right to cross the little bridge (lovely picnic area and ancient yew tree here). Climb and drop over Whit Beck and around 2.4km (1.5 miles) after High Lorton turn right onto the B5292.

⑭ KIRKSTILE INN
Loweswater CA13 0RU
01900 85219
www.kirkstile.com

⑮ MEADOW BANK
High Lorton CA13 9UG
01900 85315
meadowbanklorton.co.uk

⑯ TERRACE FARM
High Lorton CA13 9TX
01900 85278
www.terracefarm.co.uk

⑰ SWINSIDE END FARM B&B
Scales, High Lorton CA13 9UA
01900 85134   mob 07968 678530
www.swinsideendfarm.co.uk

▲ WHINFELL HALL FARM
Low Lorton CA13 0RQ
01900 85260

▲ WHEATSHEAF INN
Low Lorton CA13 9UW
01900 85199
www.wheatsheafinnlorton.co.uk

You might well see more animal than motor traffic on the country lane to Lorton

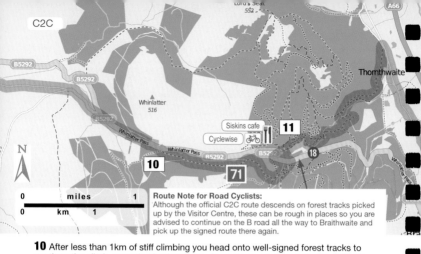

Route Note for Road Cyclists:
Although the official C2C route descends on forest tracks picked up by the Visitor Centre, these can be rough in places so you are advised to continue on the B road all the way to Braithwaite and pick up the signed route there again.

10 After less than 1km of stiff climbing you head onto well-signed forest tracks to continue the climb, emerging back onto the B road to turn left and dive back into the forest at Whinlatter Forest Park visitor centre and Siskins Cafe.

11 Just behind the main building of the visitor centre bear right. Descend the steep and bendy forest track to the road and head right into Thornthwaite.

12 Bear right onto the very minor road through Lanefoot Farm (easy to miss) and follow this road back over the B road to Ivy House and straight through Braithwaite centre.

13 Follow signs for Ullock on this very minor road, through Ullock and into Portinscale where you bear right by Derwentwater Hotel **14** and cross the river via a footbridge. Head right onto the B road (BEWARE OF TRAFFIC) and right onto the even busier A591 into Keswick centre.

18 COTTAGE IN THE WOOD
Magic Hill, Whinlatter Forest CA12 5TW
017687 78409
www.thecottageinthewood.co.uk
2 night bookings only at weekends

Note: For Thornthwaite to Portinscale accommodation entries see the Workington - Keswick chapter. For Keswick accommodation entries see the Keswick - Penrith chapter, page 47.

Brysons Cafe, Keswick

Derwentwater

Applethwaite

Thornthwaite

A66

12

Keswick Bikes

Whinlatter Bikes

A66

A591

A66

Crosthwaite Road

Whinlatter Pass

B5292

B5292

A66

B5289

Keswick

Portinscale

14

A66

Braithwaite

13

Ullock

71

B5289

Penrith Road

Borrowdale Road

Derwentwater

Lingholm Islands Derwent Isle
Lingholm Islands

The start of the
C2C in Workington

Workington ~ Keswick

Workington is still a working port and the harbour area is still dominated by heavy industry. Despite losing out to Whitehaven, with its pleasure port atmosphere, the section has advantages; it is shorter and with more gentle gradients and offers the chance to visit the lovely historic market town of Cockermouth.

The climb to Wythop Woods becomes increasingly beautiful and spectacular as you finally take to a moorland track section before dropping steeply down the thickly wooded hillside with spectacular glimpses of Bassenthwaite Lake ahead. The final section towards the handsome buildings of Keswick takes to some beautiful backroads across the Newlands Valley, only a stone's throw from Keswick but with little human traffic of any kind it really feels a world away. Keswick itself is full of diversions, from boating on Derwentwater to trying to decide which of the plethora of outdoor gear shops to browse in.

Route Info

Distance 39 km (24 miles)

Off-road 10 km (6 miles) mainly on the tarmac railpath out of Workington, but there is a very steep and stony drop to Bassenthwaite Lake that can get muddy too.

Terrain Much gentler gradients than the Whitehaven option, though there is some moderate climbing between Cockermouth and Wythop Woods but a very steep descent awaits through Wythop Woods. Take great care here and dismount if in any doubt. Careful navigation also required on the network of forest tracks. A relatively easy road section through Thornthwaite follows as you unite with the alternative start route from Whitehaven. Take care as you have to mix with busy traffic coming into Keswick.

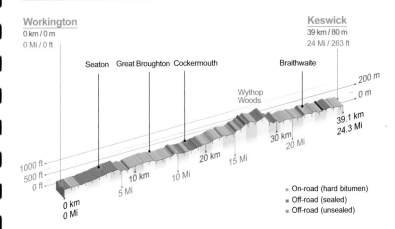

Workington
0 km / 0 m
0 Mi / 0 ft

Keswick
39 km / 80 m
24 Mi / 263 ft

Seaton   Great Broughton   Cockermouth   Braithwaite

Wythop Woods

200 m
0 m

39.1 km
24.3 Mi

30 km
20 Mi

20 km
15 Mi

10 km
10 Mi

5 Mi

1000 ft
500 ft
0 ft

0 km
0 Mi

- On-road (hard bitumen)
- Off-road (sealed)
- Off-road (unsealed)

33

What to See & Do

• Although **Workington** may look more of a working town than Whitehaven, it still has its attractions. The **Helena Thompson Museum** is based around local collections and includes social and industrial history of Workington, once world famous for coal, ship building and steel. Housed in a fine Georgian building. **Workington Hall** is an imposing ruin and former home of local Lords of the Manor the Curwens who built up the local coal industry. The hall is closed to public but its grounds and parkland are open. **Vulcan Park** is a pleasant green spot in the middle of town and has a cafe.

• **Camerton** features a pretty church on the banks of the Derwent.

• One of only two listed 'Gem Towns' in Cumbria (Whitehaven is the other), **Cockermouth** is an extremely pretty market town with interesting nooks and crannies and without the large numbers of tourists that towns nearer the centre of the Lake District attract. **Wordsworth House** was the home of William and Dorothy Wordsworth and is now National Trust owned. The **statue of R.Mayo** on main street depicts the former town MP and only Viceroy of India ever assassinated. **Jennings Brewery Tour** lets you look around a working brewery. **Castlegate House** is an art gallery and sculpture garden based around northern and Scottish artists.

In 2009 the town suffered **widespread flooding** that took many by surprise, resulting in emergency evacuations and bridges being swept away in the area and as far downstream as Workington.

For Braithwaite, Portinscale and Keswick entries see Keswick to Penrith chapter, pg 47.

The C2C entering Cockermouth gives lovely views of the market town

The C2C heads along the delightful
River Cocker in Cockermouth

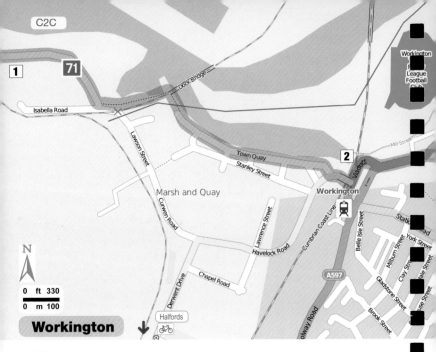

Directions

1 Start at the estuary mouth by the C2C marked building (just off the map), heading along the traffic-free path alongside the road then bending left then right, through a small harbour area, to come alongside a quay on your left (now on Town Quay).

2 Head over the railway on a bridge then turn left and swing left past the church. Take the first right onto a pavement section which continues to follow Church Street, swinging left then right onto Griffin Street to pass Allerdale council buildings. Follow this road to its end in a car park and head to the buildings in front of you (currently Opera Bingo) **3**, heading left here onto the traffic-free path. This path takes you over the Navvies Bridge and through the gated area known as Hagworm Wiggle Pass.

Accommodation

1 WAVERLEY HOTEL
Gordon Street CA14 2EN
01900 603246
www.waverley-hotel.com

2 WASHINGTON CENTRAL HOTEL
Washington Street CA14 3AY
01900 65772   washingtoncentralhotel.co.uk

3 GREEN DRAGON
Portland Square CA14 4BJ
01900 603803

4 HALL PARK HOTEL
23 Carlton Road CA14 4BX
01900 602968
thehallparkhotel.co.uk

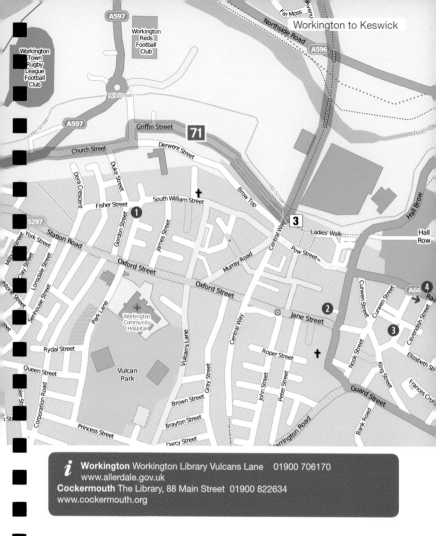

i **Workington** Workington Library Vulcans Lane 01900 706170
www.allerdale.gov.uk
Cockermouth The Library, 88 Main Street 01900 822634
www.cockermouth.org

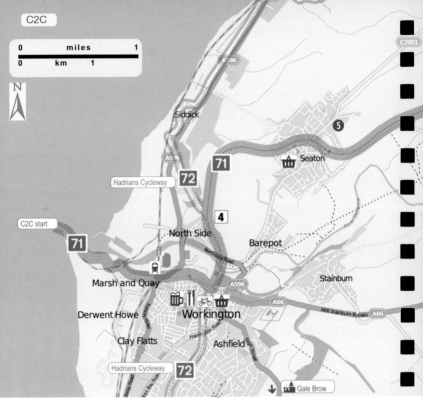

4 Around 700m (770yds) after the bridge the route splits, left heading up Hadrian's Cycleway and the Reivers routes, but you stay right. Stay on the tarmac cycle track out of Workington and into open countryside, passing over the distinctive cyclist sculpture bridge at Seaton.

5 The exit of the traffic-free path, around 5.2km (3 miles) after joining it is easy to miss, heading up a stone path before a bridge. Go right onto the road into Camerton village. Drop down through the village and take the first left turn.

6 Coming into Great Broughton turn right, signed Brigham and Cockermouth, staying on the main road through the village and descending out of it to take the second left turn signed Papcastle, 1³/₄.

5 ARMIDALE COTTAGES
29 High Seaton CA14 1PD
01900 63704 07771 768 423
www.armidalecottages.co.uk

🏕 GALE BROW
Winscales Workington CA14 4UZ
01900 873373
www.campingandcaravanningclub.co.uk

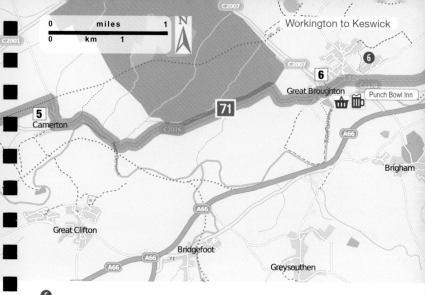

6 BROUGHTON CRAGGS HOTEL
Great Broughton CA13 0XW
01900 824400
www.broughtoncraggs.co.uk

The new flood-proof cycle and foot bridge in Workington built in the wake of devastating floods in 2009

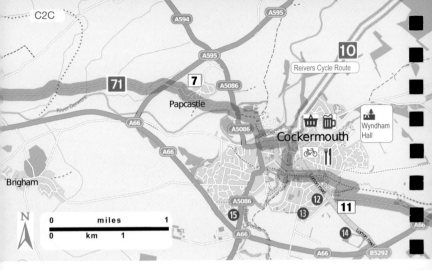

7 MANOR HOUSE HOTEL
Crown Street Cockermouth CA13 0EJ
01900 828663 www.manorcockermouth.co.uk
B&B and self-catering available

8 CROFT GUEST HOUSE
6-8 Challoner Street Cockermouth CA13 9QS
01900 827533
www.croft-guesthouse.com
2 night min Fri and Sat in summer but may waive
this - enquire by phone

9 RIVERSIDE
12 Market Place Cockermouth CA13 9NJ
01900 827504
www.riversidebedandbreakfast.co.uk

10 THE ROOK GUEST HOUSE
9 Castlegate Cockermouth CA13 9EU
01900 828496
www.therookguesthouse.co.uk

11 SIX CASTLEGATE GUESTHOUSE
6 Castlegate Cockermouth CA13 9EU
01900 826786
www.sixcastlegate.co.uk
Min 2 night stay Sats and July & Aug

12 ROSE COTTAGE
Lorton Road Cockermouth CA13 9DX
01900 822189
www.rosecottageguest.co.uk

13 BRIAR BANK B&B
14 Briar Bank Cockermouth CA13 9DN
01900 826635
www.briar-bank.co.uk

14 GRAYSONSIDE
Lorton Road Cockermouth CA13 9TQ
01900 822351   graysonside.co.uk
Note: Min stay requirements and single night
supplement may apply.

15 TRAVELODGE COCKERMOUTH
Europe Way CA13 0DJ
0871 984 6358   travelodge.co.uk

WYNDHAM HALL CARAVAN PARK
Old Keswick Road Cockermouth CA13 9SF
01900 822571
www.wyndhamholidaypark.org.uk

There are also a couple of centrally placed
luxury hotels in Cockermouth, Allerdale Court,
on Market Place and the Trout Hotel on Crown
Street.

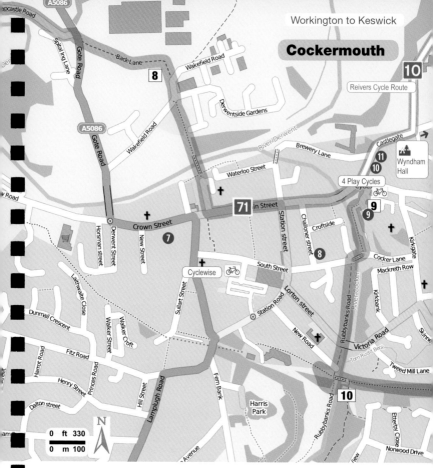

Cockermouth

Reivers Cycle Route

7 Ignore the left for Carlisle in Papcastle. Descend the hill to Cockermouth and cross Gote Road onto a rough path

8 Turn right onto a road then left onto a path and cross over the bridge to Bridge St. Go left down Main Street, cross the bridge into Market Place and right fork, then immediate right into a car park (tourist info is directly in front of you).

9 Here turn immediate right following road into the riverside car park to far end and cross the footbridge and turn left.

10 Under the second bridge turn right up the hillside and keep bearing right to cross back over the bridge you've passed under, joining the traffic-free trail. It turns from tarmac to stone, passing a large cemetery on the right then hairpins right at an NCN milepost. Go left onto the road opposite Strawberry How complex of buildings **11**.

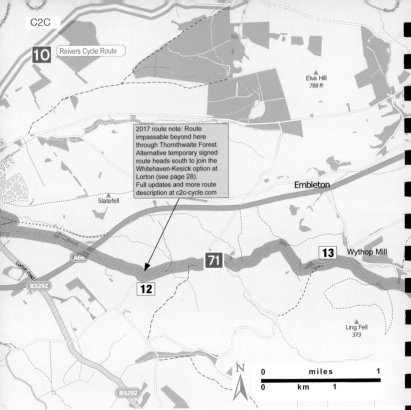

10 Reivers Cycle Route

Elva Hill
788 ft

2017 route note: Route impassable beyond here through Thornthwaite Forest. Alternative temporary signed route heads south to join the Whitehaven-Keswick option at Lorton (see page 28). Full updates and more route description at c2c-cycle.com

Embleton

Slatefell

A66

71

13 Wythop Mill

12

B5292

Lorton road

Ling Fell
373

N

| 0 | miles | 1 |
| 0 | km | 1 |

B5292

12 Head left at the next T-junction and stay on the road past a beautiful little church. Just on the edge of tiny Wythop Mill turn right before the drop **13**, and climb, passing the Old School Bunkhouse. This is now a gloriously secluded road with magnificent views. Turn right at the next junction and pass a farmhouse then head straight through gate **14** onto farm track. Go right at the track junction to descend into Wythop Woods. Follow the narrow rocky descent and cross straight over a wider, good quality track, staying on the minor path.

At the bottom of the slope go right **15** onto a minor road and straight through a bus turning circle onto lovely traffic-free old section of tarmac road.

16 Turn right at road junction and into Thornthwaite.

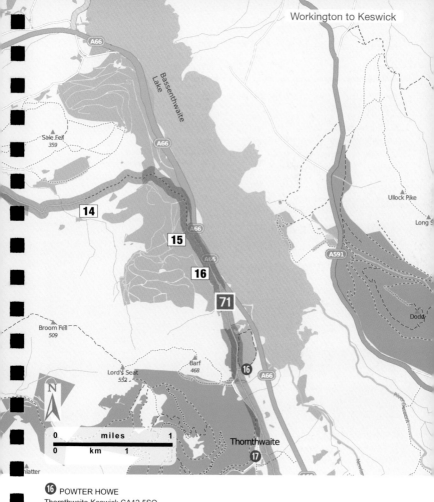

16 POWTER HOWE
Thornthwaite Keswick CA12 5SQ
017687 78415
www.powter-howe.co.uk

17 THORNTHWAITE GRANGE
Thornthwaite CA12 5SA
017687 78205 www.thornthwaite-grange.co.uk
Two night bookings only Fri & Sat May to Sept
and single night supplement.

18 BRAITHWAITE FARM
Braithwaite CA12 5RY
017687 78411
www.barnhouse-cottage.co.uk

19 MIDDLE RUDDINGS COUNTRY INN
Braithwaite CA12 5RY
017687 78436
www.middle-ruddings.co.uk
Min 2 night stay at weekends in peak season

20 RICKERBY GRANGE
Portinscale nr. Keswick CA12 5RH
017687 72344
www.rickerbygrange.co.uk
Min stay 2 nights at weekends

B CATBELLS
Low Skelgill, Newlands nr Keswick CA12 5UE
017687 78453
Min stay 2 nights at weekends

SCOTGATE HOLIDAY PARK
Braithwaite CA12 5TF
017687 78343
www.scotgateholidaypark.co.uk

Note: For Keswick accommodation entries see Keswick - Penrith chapter, pg 47.

If arriving by bike you will be using **Northern** for at least the last part of the journey, possibly a lot more if arriving from elsewhere in Northern England. Their quoted policy is 'Bikes are carried free of charge at any time and you don't need to make reservations. The cycle space on trains is clearly marked, both internally and externally. Space is allocated on a first come, first served basis. We can only carry a maximum of two bikes per train but conductors have responsibility for the safety of their train and have the right to refuse entry if the train is busy.' Tandems and other 'non-standard' bikes are likely to be excluded.
Virgin run lots of trains along the West Coast main line running through Carlisle. Bikes are carried free but an advance reservation is needed and you are supplied with a printed label. Ask a station employee in advance where your allotted space is on the train (you'll only have a few minutes to get your bike and gear aboard). TransPennine Express also use the East Coast main line and carry bikes free with reservations being made at least 24 hours in advance by calling 0345 600 1671 (option 4).

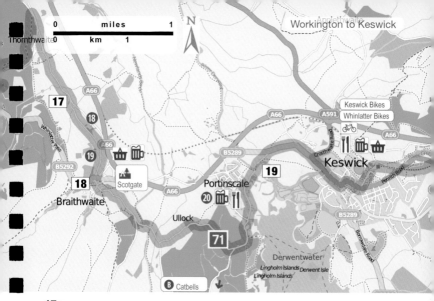

17 Bear right onto the very minor road through Lanefoot Farm (easy to miss) and follow this road back over the B5292 to Ivy House and straight through Braithwaite centre **18**. Follow signs for Ullock on this very minor road, through Ullock and into Portinscale where you bear right by the Derwentwater Hotel and cross the river via a footbridge **19**. Head right on the B road and then a busy A road into Keswick.

Keswick's bustling pedestrian centre

The C2C passes along the Greta
Valley beneath the towering mass of
Blencathra

Keswick - Penrith

The high summits of the Lake District are left behind as you approach the flatter more pastoral country of the Eden Valley, with its accent on quiet market towns and glorious woodland a real contrast to the Lake District's mass tourism. After a couple of gradients it turns into a leisurely pedal through thick woods, crossing and re-crossing the River Greta over a series of charming bridges to bring you to the picturesque village of Threlkeld. There are then some beautiful and generally very lightly trafficked roads to Greystoke, whether you take the Berrier or the Troutbeck option. The gated road to Mungrisdale has delightful views. More minor roads and tracks bring you through Newton Reigny to Penrith.

Route Info

Distance 36 km (22 miles) Taking the Old Coach Road option only adds around 1km to this total but it will feel like a lot more!

Off-road 5 miles / 8 km The Old Coach Road option is very rocky in contrast to the nice crushed stone of the Keswick railway path - the route taken by the vast majority of C2Cers. From Threlkeld it's all tarmac, with a couple of very easy cycle path sections along the A66.

Terrain Although the main route is relatively flat the off-road option along the Old Coach Road is a serious challenge as the exposed track climbs high onto Threlkeld Common, whilst the main route gently undulates along the valley bottom.
The road up to Mungrisdale features small climbs with the hills petering out almost completely as you pass through Greystoke and on to Penrith.

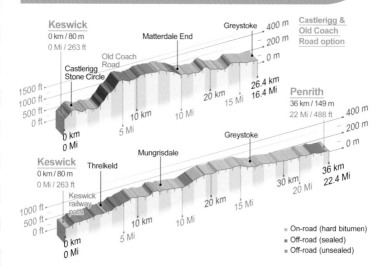

What to See & Do

• **Braithwaite** is an attractive village with pubs and a village store set in lovely surroundings.

• **Portinscale** is an elegant villa settlement next door to Keswick despite its name deriving from the Norse for prostitute's hut!

• Established as a mining centre and market town, **Keswick** quickly became a Victorian tourist centre due to its setting amidst glorious Lakeland scenery.

It remains the main tourist centre in the Northern Lakes with a number of interesting buildings including the Moot Hall and Crosthwaite Church with panoramic viewfinder. The church is the site of Romantic poet Robert Southey's grave and there are consecration crosses inside and outside the building. Keswick Museum and Art Gallery has an interesting and unusual collection of objects in a traditional museum setting whilst the Pencil Museum offers you the world's longest pencil and other offbeat pencil information. George Fisher has a huge stock of outdoor activity goods and is on Borrowdale Rd.

• **Derwentwater boat trips** sail from Keswick and call at the main points of interest around the lake.

• On a hilly route option out of Keswick, **Castlerigg Stone Circle** is a fantastic 3,000 year old stone circle amidst the towering hills. Despite the hordes who visit in summer it still has the aura of a very special place, especially as we don't really know why ancient man performed what must have been backbreaking work to build it.

• **Threlkeld** is a former mining community with TB sanitorium built nearby. Threlkeld Quarry and Mining Museum is off the B5322 south of the route.

An easy section of the Old Coach Road option (see previous page)

A haven for two-wheelers, Greystoke cyclists' cafe

• The route goes via **Mungrisdale** to Greystoke. The very basic style of Mungrisdale's church of St Kentigern suits this lonely outpost.

• **Greystoke village** has a compact centre based around a village green. There is an impressive entrance to a private castle and market cross. It also has attractions as varied as a 13th century church and a public swimming pool. Note that the local Cycle Cafe also runs a range of courses.

• Before entering **Blencow** look for the pele tower ruins with modern accommodation built into them.

• **Penrith** is a beautiful red **sandstone market town**, historically the target of Scottish border raids. Its series of market places connected by narrow streets show desire for security against the Scots. **Penrith Beacon** is a hilltop structure used through the ages to warn of the threat of invasion, the present structure dating from 1719.

Robinson's School is a former charitable provider of education now housing tourist information and small museum. The fine **St. Andrew's Church** is in Bishop's Yard. Look out for the unusual 'Giant's Grave' in the churchyard near the Gothic monument to Robert Virtue (railway engineer). The **castle**, now ruined, was begun in the fourteenth century and later occupied by Richard Duke of Gloucester as 'Guardian of the West march towards Scotland'. The **Musgrave Monument** was erected 1851 by public subscription, a memorial on the early death of Sir George and Lady Musgrave's son. Penrith has many other fine buildings such as the Mansion House and Town Hall.

Out of town, about 2 miles south-west of the route you is **Rheged**, Europe's biggest grass-covered building with giant cinema and plenty of shops and eating places.

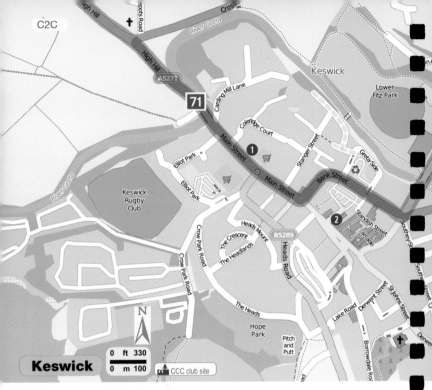

Accommodation

1 THE KINGS ARMS HOTEL
Main Street CA12 5BL
0800 8401241 lakedistricthotels.net/kingsarms

2 INN ON THE SQUARE
Market Square CA12 5JF
0800 8401247
www.innonthesquare.co.uk

3 CARTWHEEL B&B
5 Blencathra Street CA12 4HW
017687 73182 thecartwheel.co.uk

4 GLENCOE GUEST HOUSE
21 Helvellyn Street CA12 4EN
017687 71016
www.glencoeguesthouse.co.uk

5 GRASSMOOR GUEST HOUSE
10 Blencathra Street CA12 4HP
017687 74008 grassmoor-keswick.co.uk

5 CRANFORD HOUSE
18 Eskin Street CA12 4DG
017687 71017 cranfordhouse.co.uk

6 BECKSIDE GUEST HOUSE
5 Wordsworth Street CA12 4HU
017687 73093
www.beckside-keswick.co.uk

7 LINNETT HILL
4 Penrith Road Keswick CA12 4HF
017687 44518
www.linnetthillhotel.com

8 TWA DOGS INN
Penrith Road CA12 4JU
017687 72599
www.twadogs.co.uk

H KESWICK YOUTH HOSTEL
Station Road CA12 5LH
0345 371 9746
www.yha.org.uk

H DENTON HOUSE
Penrith Rd CA12 4JW
01768 775351
dentonhouse-keswick.co.uk

CAMPING AND CARAVANNING CLUB SITE
Crow Park Road CA12 5EP
017687 72392
www.campingandcaravanningclub.co.uk

There is a vast choice of accommodation in
Keswick and if all listings here are full a stroll
along Bank Street, Station Street, Station Road
and Penrith Road should reveal plenty more
choices.

Directions

1 You enter Keswick on the main road and follow Bank Street and Station Road to the
car park by the swimming pool and the start of the railpath to Threlkeld. The railpath
passes over the river and the main road.

❾ LAUREL BANK
Penrith Road CA12 4LJ
017687 73006
www.laurelbankkeswick.co.uk

**⛺ CASTLERIGG HALL CARAVAN
& CAMPING PARK**
Keswick CA12 4TE
017687 74499 www.castlerigg.co.uk

⛺ CASTLERIGG FARM
CA12 4TE
017687 72479 www.castleriggfarm.com

⛺ BURNS FARM
St Johns-in-the-Vale CA12 4RR
017687 79112 www.burns-farm.co.uk

Ⓗ DERWENTWATER YOUTH HOSTEL
Barrow House Borrowdale
Keswick CA12 5UR
017687 77246 www.derwentwater.org

VALLEY BOTTOM (RAILPATH) OPTIONS
2 Continue under two more main roads using the impressive stilted boardwalk which has now replaced the old and troublesome steps over the former railway tunnel.
3 After a couple of miles bear left on the road into Threlkeld.

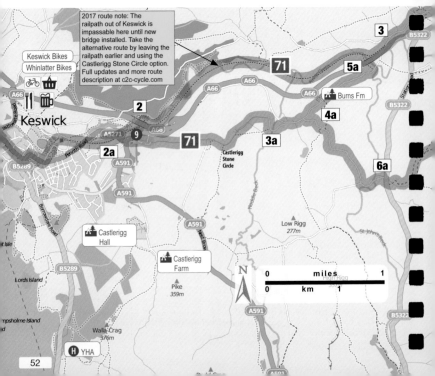

2017 route note: The railpath out of Keswick is impassable here until new bridge installed. Take the alternative route by leaving the railpath earlier and using the Castlerigg Stone Circle option. Full updates and more route description at c2c-cycle.com

CASTLERIGG STONE CIRCLE / OLD COACH ROAD OPTION

Pick up the railpath out of Keswick as described on the previous pages. You will need to exit the Keswick-Threlkeld railpath just before it first passes under a main road, some 0.85km (0.5 miles) after joining it **2a**. Head up the hill and soon turn left, signed Penrith /Workington A66 then very shortly take the next right onto a minor road signed for Castlerigg Stone Circle and climb steeply to this wonderful ancient site.

Descend past the climbing centre, heading right in the valley bottom and cross Naddle Beck **3a**.

4a Take the next right signed St Johns in the Vale if carrying on to the Old Coach Road, or head straight on if looping back to the railpath, which you can rejoin in just over 1km (0.75 miles) by heading left on the track through the woods **5a**, just opposite a small house at the bottom of a descent.

If heading for the challenge of the Old Coach Road simply follow this lovely winding road along the valley of St. Johns in the Vale, passing a right turn to the church and Youth Centre, just before crossing St Johns Beck. Meeting the B5322 **6a** go right and almost immediate left, signed Matterdale, to join the start of the track known as the Old Coach Road.

Navigation on this option is not difficult - but it is a real physical test and I have yet to see anyone actually cycling (as opposed to pushing) up the entire length of the Old Coach Road's bouldery climb.

Breathtaking views and a breathtaking challenge; the Old Coach Road option

4 Through Threlkeld pick up a lovely old road above the valley (now closed to traffic), dropping down to the cycleway alongside the A66 for a mile or so then pick up the road at Scales (for unsigned shortcut option see * below).
5 From Scales the official signed route follows an undulating climb along a gated road that leads to the Mill Inn on the edge of Mungrisdale village **6**. Over the Glenderamackin river head right signed for Keswick, and follow the fast wide road back down to the A66. **7** At the A66 go left onto another section of cycleway by the trunk road.

* UNSIGNED SHORT-CUT OPTION
5 At Scales drop down to the A66, jinking left then right across it, taking great care, very shortly going right for Wallthwaite. Follow the road, ignoring any turnings, and come back to the A66, and head right onto the cycle lane on the far side of it to rejoin the signed route **6**. This cuts well over 3 miles off the route and is a much flatter option.

⑩ HORSE & FARRIER INN
Threlkeld CA12 4SQ
017687 79688
www.horseandfarrier.com

⑪ THE SALLY
Threlkeld CA12 4SQ
017687 79614   www.thesalutation.co.uk

⑫ SCALES FARM COUNTRY GUEST HOUSE
Scales Threlkeld CA12 4SY
017687 79660 Mob 07971 853360
www.scalesfarm.com
Min stay requirement at times / single night supplement

Ⓑ WHITE HORSE INN
Scales CA12 4SY
017687 79883
www.thewhitehorse-blencathra.co.uk
May be a minimum 2 night stay if booking Sats - enquire. Can advise on camping options locally.

🏕 TROUTBECK CAMPING AND CARAVANNING CLUB SITE
Hutton Moor End Troutbeck CA11 0SX
01768 779149
troutbeckcaravanpark.co.uk
Winter closing, two night min stay in high season

Scales

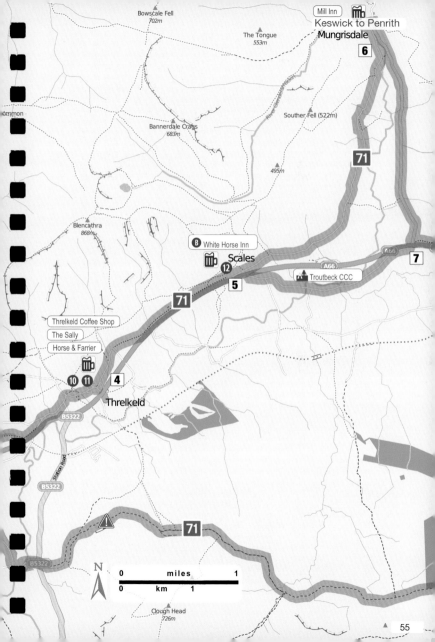

Mill Inn
Mungrisdale
6

Bowscale Fell
702m

The Tongue
553m

Souther Fell (522m)

ommon

Bannerdale Crags
683m

71

495m

Blencathra
868m

ⓑ White Horse Inn

Scales
12

71
5

A66

A66

Troutbeck CCC
7

Threlkeld Coffee Shop

The Sally

Horse & Farrier

10 **11** **4**

Threlkeld

B5322

Station Road

B5322

⚠

71

B5322

N

0	miles	1
0	km	1

Clough Head
726m

55

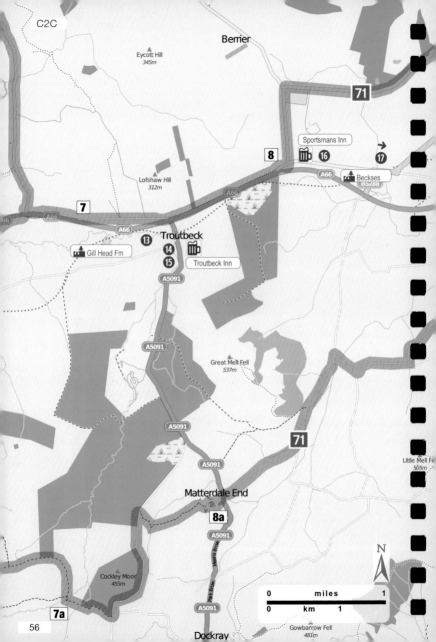

C2C

Berrier

Eycott Hill
345m

71

Sportsmans Inn

8   🍺 16   →17

A66   🏕 Beckses
B5288

Lofshaw Hill
312m

7   A66

Gill Head Fm   13 Troutbeck
14 🍺
15 Troutbeck Inn

A5091

A5091

Great Mell Fell
537m

A5091

71

Little Mell Fell
505m

A5091

Matterdale End

8a

A5091

Cockley Moor
455m

N

| 0 | miles | 1 |
| 0 | km | 1 |

7a

56

Dockray

Gowbarrow Fell
481m

VALLEY BOTTOM OPTION

7 The cycle lane by the A66 switches onto a long straight road parallel to the A66 emerging again at the A66 opposite Troutbeck.

8 Shortly you leave the A66 again, turning left at the Sportsman Inn. It's now easy navigation on quiet roads, turning right past Hopkinsons Caravan Park, which turns into a wonderful freewheeling descent towards Greystoke.

OLD COACH ROAD OPTION

Once over the crest the track quality improves significantly and you are on a steady downhill run, making for a glorious ride across open moorland with wonderful expansive views. Across the lovely little waterfall at Grove Beck **7a** you are soon back on road before another short track section to the farming hamlet of Matterdale End **8a** where you pick up a well-signed quiet road route. This joins the B5288 (see overleaf) where you head right into Greystoke.

13 LANE HEAD FARM
Troutbeck CA11 0SY
017687 79220
www.laneheadfarm.co.uk
Min 2 night stay at weekends, 3 at Bank Holidays

14 TROUTBECK INN
Troutbeck CA11 0SJ
017684 83635
www.troutbeckinn.co.uk
Some minimum stay restrictions

15 NETHERDENE
Troutbeck CA11 0SJ
017687 483475
www.netherdene.co.uk
Note: 2 night min stay waived for C2Cers; please
call if you have problems booking online

16 WHITBARROW FARM
Berrier CA11 0XB
017684 83366
www.whitbarrowfarm.co.uk

17 MOTHERBY HOUSE
Motherby CA11 0RJ
017684 83368
www.motherbyhouse.co.uk

GILL HEAD FARM
Troutbeck Penrith CA11 0ST (017687) 79652
www.gillheadfarm.co.uk
Camping, camping pods and gypsy wagons

BECKSES CARAVAN & CAMPING PARK
Penruddock Penrith CA11 0RX
017684 83224 www.theaa.com

Spectacularly located camping at Gill Head Farm

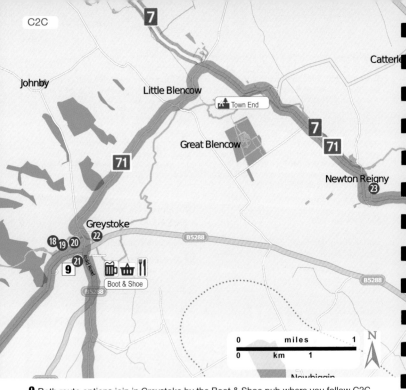

9 Both route options join in Greystoke by the Boot & Shoe pub where you follow C2C signs for Penrith. It is now easy navigation through the villages of Little Blencow, Laithes and Newton Reigny (shortly after Little Blencow the C2C follows NCN 7, leaving NCN 71 behind).

i **Penrith** Middlegate 01768 867466 www.visiteden.co.uk

 Penrith station is on the West Coast mainline and so has regular, quick services north to Glasgow and south to London (some direct services and some changing at Lancaster).

Services are run by Transpennine Express (see page 22 for cycle carriage details) and Virgin, whose trains have space for up to 4 bikes (2 tandems on Pendolino trains). Reservations are free but compulsory and part of the fully automated ticket booking process (also available on 03445 565650). Both Voyager and Pendolino trains carry a yellow rectangle at the opposite end to the bike space. This is usually at the 'country' (ie furthest from London) end of the train.

18 BEECH HOUSE
Berrier Road Greystoke CA11 0UE
017684 80829
www.beechhousegreystoke.co.uk

19 ORCHARD COTTAGE
Church Road Greystoke CA11 0TW
017684 83264
www.bandborchardcottagegreystoke.co.uk

20 STAFFORD HOUSE
Greystoke Penrith CA11 0TQ
017684 83558
www.stafford-house.co.uk
B 🏕 by arrangement

21 BOOT & SHOE PUB
Greystoke CA11 0TP
017684 83343
www.bootandshoegreystoke.co.uk

22 THE BRATHEN
The Thorpe Greystoke CA11 0TJ
017684 83595
www.brathen.co.uk
B&B and self-catering cottage available

23 SUNSET HOUSE
Newton Reigny CA11 0AY
01768 895629 / 07391517835
www.sunsethousebb.co.uk

🏕 TOWN END COTTAGE CARAVAN CLUB
SITE & CAMP SITE
Laithes CA11 0AW
017684 84317

The ever popular Boot & Shoe in Greystoke village

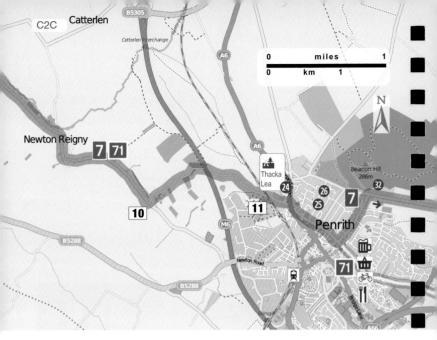

24 ACORN GUEST HOUSE
Scotland Road Penrith CA11 9HL
01768 868696 www.acorn-guesthouse.co.uk

25 NORCROFT GUEST HOUSE
Graham Street Penrith CA11 9LQ
01768 862365 www.norcroft-guesthouse.co.uk
Full C2C service backup (bike and luggage
transport, return to route start etc).

26 BANK HOUSE
Graham Street Penrith CA11 9LE
01768 868714 www.bankhousepenrith.co.uk

27 BRANDELHOW GUEST HOUSE
1 Portland Place CA11 7QN
01768 864470
www.brandelhowguesthouse.co.uk

28 BROOKLANDS GUEST HOUSE
2 Portland Place CA11 7QN
01768 863395 www.brooklandsguesthouse.com

29 ALBANY HOUSE
5 Portland Place CA11 7QN
01768 863072 www.albany-house.org.uk

30 STATION HOTEL
Castlegate CA11 7JB
01768 866714 www.stationpenrith.co.uk

31 CALEDONIA GUEST HOUSE
8, Victoria Road CA11 8HR
01768 864482
www.caledoniaguesthouse.co.uk

32 ROUNDTHORN COUNTRY HOUSE
Beacon Edge Penrith CA11 7HA
01768 863952 www.roundthorn.co.uk

H WAYFARERS HOSTEL
19 Brunswick Square Penrith CA11 7LR
01768 866011 www.wayfarershostel.com
Bike hire and workshop

THACKA LEA
Thacka Lane Penrith CA11 9HX
01768 863319

For more choice there are numerous B&Bs along
Graham Street, Portland Place, Castlegate and
Victoria Road.

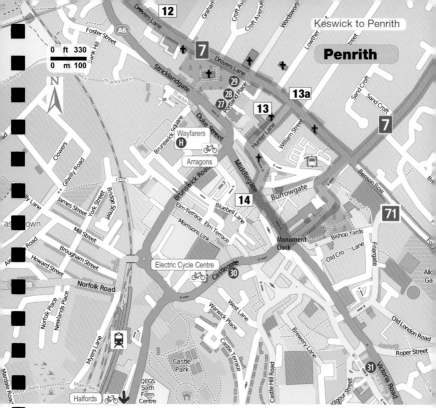

10 About half a mile out of Newton Reigny turn left at the Millennium Milepost and pass through the college buildings at Newton Rigg, using the public bridleway link to come under the M6 bridge. Turn right at a T-junction here and follow the track under the railway **11**.

The track becomes Robinson Street and at the end you cross a main road onto Drovers Lane (using the contraflow cycle lane) **12**. Follow this road for about 150 yards, over a roundabout, You now have two options:

13 If visiting the attractive town centre then head right down Hunter Lane towards Penrith centre. Follow Hunter Lane and take the last left down Queen Street to bring you out on the main street **14**. Go left here along the main street up to the Monument clock, the heart of Penrith.

13a If by-passing the town centre ignore Hunter Lane and carry straight on down Meeting House Lane to pass the bus station and head left up Fell Lane.

See page 69 for directions exiting Penrith.

The descent to Leadgate is accompanied by
sweeping views across the Northern Pennines

Penrith ~ Nenthead

Leave Penrith behind on a long, steady climb up to some spectacular Lakeland views from Beacon Edge. Leaving the gentle Eden Valley behind, you soon climb steeply to the spectacular viewpoint of Hartside ('extreme' off-road options up to here for cycling masochists only!) before beginning the traverse of the Northern Pennines, 'England's Last Wilderness', much of it designated an Area of Outstanding Natural Beauty. Though lacking the alpine quality of the lakes, the sombre, wide open spaces present, if anything, a more powerful landscape and there are certainly fewer settlements and chances for refreshment.

At tiny Leadgate you have the option of a lovely quiet ride down the South Tyne valley to delightful Garrigill then a steep but spectacular climb and drop to Nenthead, or the comparative plethora of restaurants and pubs in the characterful Pennine town of Alston (self-proclaimed highest market town in England), which involves a leveller but less spectacular ride on an A-road.

Route Info

Distance 43 km (27 miles)

Off - road 6.5km (4 miles) At Four Lane End, east of Renwick, the off-road option up Hartside splits from the road route but be warned, this option is very rough, bouldery and uses often very steep countryside tracks in the main, so is not really recommended. For the slight distance it saves it adds much more in time and effort (hence we don't mark it on the map here).

The off-road option between Garrigill and Nenthead is a challenge but good fun; it includes some very steep, rocky rough stuff suitable for more experienced off-roaders only as you climb out of the South Tyne valley away from Garrigill, but once on the moorland track past Priorsdale it's a much more rideable affair as it levels out and the surface improves (fattish tyres recommended). There's a small section with a rockier surface passing the old Nenthead mines just before the village. You should be aware of potentially extreme weather conditions if crossing this part of the route November - April.

Terrain From Penrith to Renwick there are plenty of relatively small ups and downs as you cross the Eden Valley. Two of the C2C's major climbs feature here, the ascent of Hartside and the climb between Garrigill and Nenthead, should you opt for this route instead of the Alston alternative. The Alston option involves much less climbing than the Garrigill option but means more mixing with fast traffic on the A689 to Nenthead.

Other A road options requiring some care are the approach to Langwathby and either side of Hartside where you should keep an eagle eye out for motorbikers screaming past you (the A689 across the Pennines is one of the most popular motorbikers' routes in the whole country).

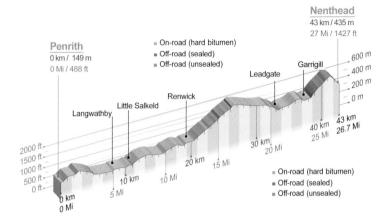

Penrith
0 km / 149 m
0 Mi / 488 ft

Nenthead
43 km / 435 m
27 Mi / 1427 ft

- On-road (hard bitumen)
- Off-road (sealed)
- Off-road (unsealed)

Garrigill

Leadgate

Renwick

Langwathby

Little Salkeld

600 m
400 m
200 m
0 m

2000 ft
1500 ft
1000 ft
500 ft
0 ft

0 km
0 Mi

5 Mi

10 km

10 Mi

20 km

15 Mi

30 km

20 Mi

40 km

25 Mi

43 km
26.7 Mi

- On-road (hard bitumen)
- Off-road (sealed)
- Off-road (unsealed)

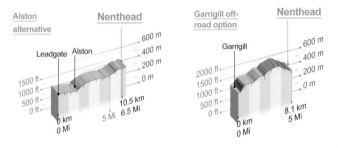

Alston alternative   **Nenthead**

Leadgate   Alston

600 m
400 m
200 m
0 m

1500 ft
1000 ft
500 ft
0 ft

0 km
0 Mi

5 Mi

10.5 km
6.5 Mi

Garrigill off-road option   **Nenthead**

Garrigill

600 m
400 m
200 m
0 m

2000 ft
1500 ft
1000 ft
500 ft
0 ft

0 km
0 Mi

8.1 km
5 Mi

The lovely approach to Garrigill from Leadgate

What to See & Do

• The compact village of **Langwathby** is centred around the village green.

• A couple of miles on at **Little Salkeld** there is a nice walk to Lacey's Caves and a water-powered mill produces organic flours.

• Just up the road **Long Meg and her Daughters** is an impressive prehistoric stone circle with a large megalith at the head and made up of 60 stones of 360 ft diameter. The purpose is unsure but it has possible funerary connections. Little Meg is a smaller circle to the north with no public access. Long Meg is a very short detour from the C2C as it climbs out of Little Salkeld.

• Your tough climb out of the Eden Valley is rewarded with a superb 580m viewpoint, **Hartside**, and its accompanying cafe. The **North Pennines Area of Outstanding Natural Beauty** which looks barren actually harbours a unique blend of flora, fauna (e.g. alpine flowers and birds such as the merlin) and industrial archaeology. The great northern rivers the Tyne, Tees, Wear and Derwent rise here. Several hills are crossed but the area is a single mass of ancient rock, covered mainly in peat, 40 by 36 miles.

• **Garrigill** is a very picturesque village. The Blacksmith's Forge and Waterfalls Walk are on the road route leaving Garrigill. Like Nenthead further on, it has a great range of services for such a small place; village shop and post office, a lovely pub, a good stock of varied accommodation and even a swimming pool. **Ashgill Force** is a fifty foot waterfall near Garrigill you can stand behind. Access on foot only.

Long Meg and her daughters, a short detour off the route

• The **Alston** route option wasn't on the original C2C route but it is now signed and mapped, providing an alternative between Leadgate and Nenthead. It lies at the junction of two 'A' roads and therefore you will have some relatively heavy traffic to face, but there are more facilities available than in Garrigill or Nenthead.

Alston claims to be England's **highest market town** at 280m (919ft). Its greatest period of growth was based on a largely **Quaker-owned lead mining industry**. During its heyday in the nineteenth century the town had a population of 10,000 but is now down to 2,000. It boasts many **old attractive buildings**, mainly nineteenth century, which attracted the media to make a TV version of Oliver Twist. It is also a regional centre for artists and craftspeople. The **parish church** is one of the most notable buildings, featuring the Derwentwater clock. Greenwich Hospital gained large estates in the area and gave the clock to the church.

• **South Tynedale Railway** is England's highest narrow gauge railway and runs for 2.25 miles along former BR track here providing a 15 minute trip through great scenery.

• The **Nent Force drainage level** began in Alston and was over four miles long when work ceased and took 60 years to build. It became a tourist attraction in the nineteenth century with boat trips and underground dancing! After extraction and smelting the lead was carried away by sturdy Galloway ponies.

Alston has some fine old buildings

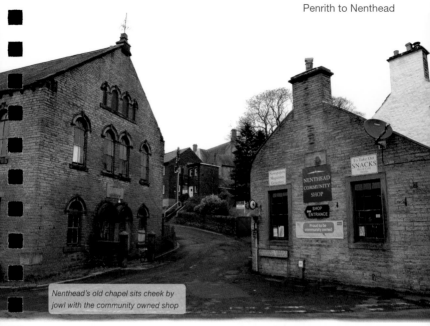

Nenthead's old chapel sits cheek by jowl with the community owned shop

• **Nenthead** is a former mining settlement. Set amidst wild Pennine scenery, it claims to be England's highest village. During winter travellers to Allendale found a journey through the mines easier than going 'over the tops'. Originally a **planned settlement for mine workers** (1825), it was organised by the same Quaker-based London Lead Company predominant in Alston. Working conditions for the time were good and included provision of public baths and pension funds. A **reading room** and impressive **village hall** still remain. The well-preserved **Methodist church** reflects the former strength of religion. The ornate **fountain** is a memorial to R.W. Bainbridge, superintendent of the mine company.

Today it still thrives with a host of locally run businesses providing an oasis of hospitality amidst the wilds. **North Pennine Cycles** has been a lifeline for many C2Cers with bikes needing repair or adjustment whilst the Miners Arms pub doubles as a B&B, the Overwater Lodge restaurant lets you celebrate being at the highest point on the route (well, almost) and the village shop is a much valued community enterprise. The lovely chapel at the centre of the village was the subject of a lottery award and North Pennine Cycles plan to expand into it from its current site in the old post office.
• **Nenthead mines'** 200 acres has numerous remnants of lead and silver mining. Heritage centre has one or two open days a month over the summer.

The wonderfully peaceful off-road
option between Garrigill and Nenthead

Directions

1 From Monument Clock in Penrith centre head down the path between NatWest and Barclays (dismount here). After 150 yards go left and right in 50 yards after the car park, heading to the mini-roundabout at the top of Sandgate. Head right then almost immediately take a left onto Fell Lane.
Climb Fell Lane and go right onto Beacon Edge **2**.
3 Take the first left turn off Beacon Edge and descend down a steep hill to the B6412 and right onto it. In less than half a mile go right to meet the main A686 turning left onto it **4**.

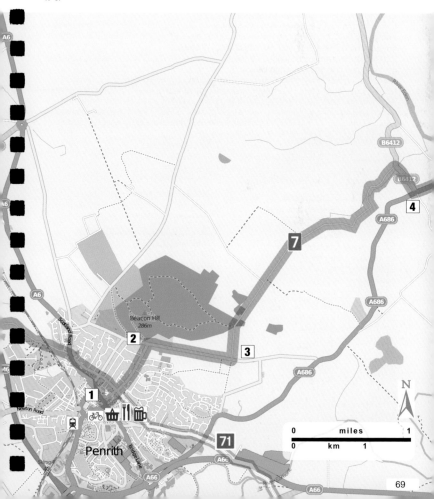

5 Cross the River Eden on a footbridge to come into Langwathby. Take the first left off the main road in Langwathby at the war memorial, passing the pub, post office and church to exit the village. Follow the road out of Langwathby and in 1.5 miles climb steeply through Little Salkeld (detour to Long Meg to left 1 mile out of Little Salkeld - worth a visit).

Back on the main route take the second right at the next junction, signed Gamblesby and Alston **6** (*though you could detour here to Kirkoswald and Lazonby - see below). Take the next left. Straight across the crossroads **7** descend over Hazlerigg Beck and continue on the lovely road over Viol Moor to Four Lane End (see map overleaf for Four Lane End).

UNOFFICIAL DETOUR VIA KIRKOSWALD / LAZONBY

If you want to visit the lovely village of Kirkoswald, with its three pubs and shop, or the swimming pool at Lazonby or one of the campsites in either village, it could be worth the extra 8km (5 miles) or so for a trip via both villages.

At the Gamblesby / Alston junction **6** marked * above don't go right but stay on the road as it bends left and follow it into Glassonby.

Both villages are signed from Glassonby and you come into Kirkoswald by the unusual looking pele tower **7a** (a mini-fortress designed to defend against the Scots). Lazonby is a there and back trip from Kirkoswald and back in Kirkoswald you take the signed Alston turning along a lovely undulating road parallel to Raven Beck, rejoining the main C2C at Four Lane End, going left for the road route (map overleaf for Four Lane End).

Accommodation

1 EDENHALL COUNTRY HOUSE
Edenhall CA11 8SX
01768 881454   www.edenhallhotel.co.uk

2 B BANK HOUSE FARM
Little Salkeld Langwathby CA10 1NN
01768 881257
www.c2c-cycle-accommodation.co.uk

3 MARION LODGE
Little Salkeld CA10 1NW
01768 881745 07920 180305
marionlodgebookings@gmail.com

4 LAZONBY HALL
Lazonby CA10 1AZ
01768 870300
www.lazonbyhall.co.uk

B MAINS FARM
Kirkoswald CA10 1DH   01768 898342
www.edenvalleycaravansite.co.uk

LAZONBY SWIMMING POOL AND
CARAVAN SITE
Lazonby CA10 1BL
01768 898346
www.lazonbypool.co.uk

Langwathby village

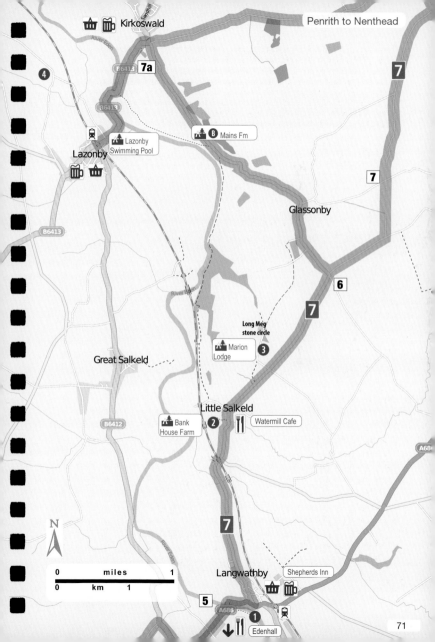

Kirkoswald

7a

7

4

Lazonby
Swimming Pool

Lazonby

B Mains Fm

Glassonby

7

B6413

6

Long Meg
stone circle

7

Great Salkeld

Marion
Lodge **3**

Little Salkeld

2

Bank
House Farm

Watermill Cafe

A68

7

N

Langwathby

Shepherds Inn

0　　miles　　1
0　　km　　1

5

A686

1

Edenhall

8 At Four Lane End where the off-road option heads off to the right (extremely rough and not a practical option for most), head straight on to Renwick, where you bear right twice in quick succession, skirting the village, to begin the long spectacular climb to Hartside. Watch out for the Pennine Cycleway joining from the right **9**, then the climbing begins in earnest, with spectacular views behind you across the Eden Valley to the peaks of Lakeland. You cross the increasingly unrideable off-road option **10** to join the A686 and head left **11**, with most riders pushing up the last little bit of off-road route to Hartside motorbikers cafe at the summit, cutting off the final hairpin **12**.

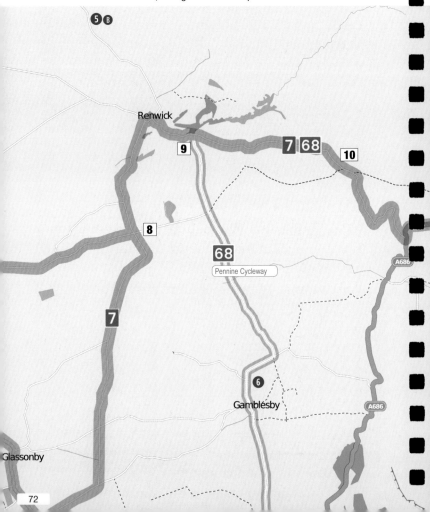

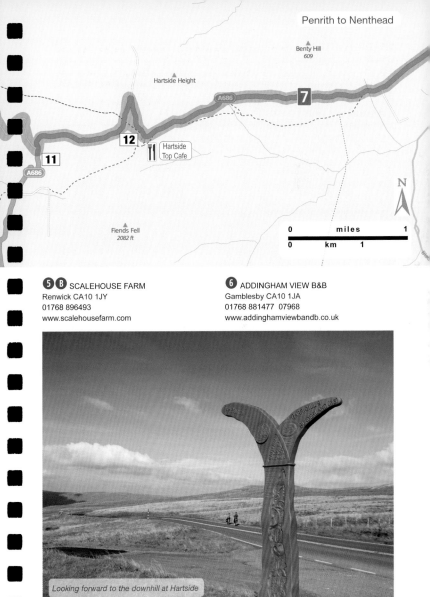

Benty Hill
609

Hartside Height ▲

A686

7

12

Hartside
Top Cafe

11

A686

N

Fiends Fell ▲
2082 ft

0	miles	1
0	km	1

5 B SCALEHOUSE FARM
Renwick CA10 1JY
01768 896493
www.scalehousefarm.com

6 ADDINGHAM VIEW B&B
Gamblesby CA10 1JA
01768 881477 07968
www.addinghamviewbandb.co.uk

Looking forward to the downhill at Hartside

13 Nearly 5km (3 miles) after the Hartside summit split off right onto a minor road descent, signed Leadgate and Garrigill.

14 At the T-junction in Leadgate you must choose between the Garrigill option to the right (lovely minor roads and a great off-road option) and the Alston option (heavier traffic but a greater choice of pubs and restaurants).

ALSTON ALTERNATIVE
Navigation is a cinch - meet the A686 and turn right **15a**, coming into Alston. Cross the river and, shortly, look out for the lovely main street, climbing to your right.

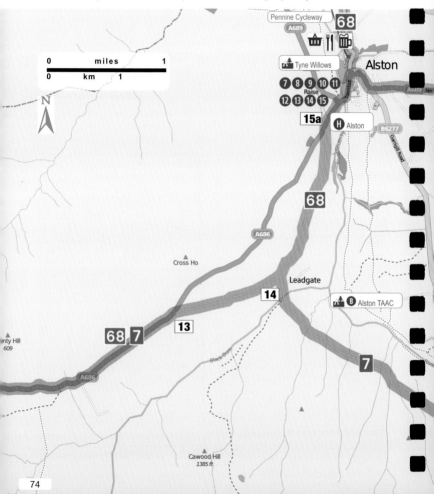

7 VICTORIA INN
Front Street Alston CA9 3SE
01434 381194

8 ANGEL INN
Front Street Alston CA9 3HU
01434 381363

9 CUMBERLAND HOTEL
Townfoot Alston CA9 3HX
01434 381875
www.cumberlandalston.co.uk

10 ALSTON HOUSE HOTEL
Townfoot Alston CA9 3RN
01434 382200
www.alstonhousehotel.co.uk

11 TOWN VIEW
Market Place Alston CA9 3HS
01434 382534 / 07903 923300
www.townviewalston.co.uk

12 HARBUT LAW
Brampton Road Alston CA9 3BD
01434 381950
www.cumbria-cottages.co.uk

13 HIGHFIELDS
Bruntley Meadows Alston CA9 3UX
01434 382182
kalinkaleo@gmail.com

14 GREYCROFT
1 Middle Park The Raise Alston CA9 3AR
01434 381383
www.greycroftalston.co.uk

15 LOWBYER MANOR COUNTRY HOUSE
Hexham Road Alston CA9 3JX
01434 381230
www.lowbyer.com

H ALSTON YOUTH HOSTEL
The Firs Alston CA9 3RW
01434 381509
www.yha.org.uk

 B ALSTON TRAINING AND ADVENTURE
CENTRE
High Plains Lodge Alston CA9 3DD
01434 381886
www.alstontraining.co.uk
South of Alston along the B6277

 TYNE WILLOWS
Station Road Alston
01434 382515

i **Alston** Town Hall Alston 01434 382244 www.visiteden.co.uk

Langwathby has a station on the Settle-Carlisle line, one of the most
scenic lines in the country. It has direct connections to Leeds and Carlisle.
If you need to bail out of the C2C at Alston just follow NCN 68 (Pennine Cycleway)
north for 22 km (13.5 miles), much of it easy traffic-free trail, to Haltwhistle station
where you can head east to Newcastle or west back to Workington or Whitehaven.

GARRIGILL - NENTHEAD ON-ROAD OPTION

15 At the George and Dragon pub in Garrigill turn left (* right for off-road option - see below) and just before the lovely waterfall and chapel turn right to climb steeply. Head straight over the next crossroads **16** as the climb levels out and crosses the rather dour surroundings of Flinty Fell.

A very steep descent into Nenthead brings you to a T-junction **17**. Go right here, passing Overwater Lodge restaurant and come to the main A689 opposite the Miners Arms and bike shop and village shop **18**.

GARRIGILL - NENTHEAD OFF-ROAD OPTION

15 At the George and Dragon pub in Garrigill bear right. Pass the church on the left and then look out for a wooden fingerpost signed as a public way to Pasture House. Head across the river on a concrete ford and climb very steeply up a rubbly track before the surface improves and turns to tarmac before meeting the B6277.

16a Go right on the B road here and in 1.5km (nearly 1 mile), go left, signed on a fingerpost for Priorsdale, immediately passing Mid-Ashgill cottage.

The tarmac climbs then drops through a forestry plantation (nice waterfall here) then bears left **17a** to become a wonderful moorland track of compacted stone. Finally a short rubbly descent leads through Nenthead Mines Centre, emerging at a road in Nenthead. Join the on-road option by going right here, to the A689 **18**.

16 LOVELADY SHIELD
Lovelady Lane Alston CA9 3LX
01434 381203
www.lovelady.co.uk

17 NENT HALL COUNTRY HOUSE HOTEL
Alston CA9 3LQ
01434 381584
www.nenthall.com
Self catering cottage available

18 GARRIGILL POST OFFICE GUEST HOUSE
Garrigill CA9 3DS
01434 381257
www.garrigill-guesthouse.co.uk
Seasonal opening

19 EASTVIEW
Garrigill CA9 3DU
01434 381561
wwwgarrigillbedandbreakfast.co.uk

20 ENNERDALE HOUSE HOLIDAY COTTAGE
Garrigill CA9 3DY
01434 382119
www.holidayingarrigill.co.uk
Self catering cottage

21 MINERS ARMS
Nenthead CA9 3PF
01434 381427
www.nenthead.com

22 CHERRY TREE COTTAGE
Nenthead CA9 3PD
01434 381434
www.cherrytree-cottage.org

B HUDGILL CARAVAN PARK
Nr Nenthall, Alston CA9 3LG
07754 650038

B HAGGS BANK BUNKHOUSE
Haggs Bank Mine Shop
Nentsbury Alston CA9 3LH
07919 092403
haggsbank.com/bunkhouse

B MILL COTTAGE BUNKHOUSE
Nenthead
01434 381674   millcottagebunkhouse.co.uk

B ASSAY HOUSE BUNKHOUSE
Nenthead Mines
01388527532   admin@nentheadmines.com
www.nentheadmines.com/category/bunkhouse

B GARRIGILL VILLAGE HALL
01434 647516
www.garrigillvh.org.uk

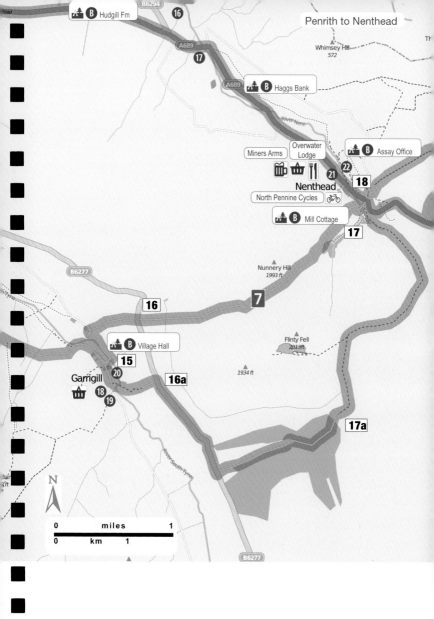

Whimsey Hill
572

B6294

16

A689

17

A689

Haggs Bank

River Nent

Miners Arms

Overwater Lodge

Assay Office

22

21

18

Nenthead

North Pennine Cycles

Mill Cottage

17

Nunnery Hill
1993 ft

B6277

16

7

Flinty Fell
2013 ft

Village Hall

15

1934 ft

20

16a

Garrigill

18

19

17a

River South Tyne

N

0	miles	1
0	km	1

B6277

Hudgill Fm

Muggleswick Common as seen from the Waskerley Way

Nenthead ~ Consett

You experience the highest point on the route during this section, Black Hill, at 609 metres (1998 feet) so be prepared for the possibility of extreme weather.

Lead mining villages such as Nenthead, Allenheads and Rookhope have a curious collection of mining relics such as the Lintzgarth Arch and Bolt's Law Standing Engine. Larger settlements are strung along Weardale Valley and a C2C route option passes through one of the largest of them, Stanhope. It too is a real one off, boasting attractions as various as an outdoor swimming pool and a fossilised tree! Fine sweeping vistas along the traffic-free Waskerley Way lead to the magnificent Hownsgill viaduct and Consett where the route splits to Sunderland or Tynemouth.

Route Info

Distance 45 km (28 miles)

Off - road 30 km (18 miles), including the Rookhope off-road option. The small short cut off-road option out of Nenthead is reasonable quality crushed stone. A stony, steep and uneven climb heads to the grouse moor above Rookhope where a stony track is better quality but still pretty bumpy. The final 3.5 km / 2 miles is on a grassy and very uneven track that is really mountain bike territory. The Waskerley Way is pretty well surfaced and should pose few problems whatever bike you are on.

Terrain

The Rookhope off-road moorland route is most direct with least climbing but it means bumpy and very rutted tracks. Stanhope road option is longer but with a very steep, extended climb. Options join at the Waskerley Way then it's downhill to the coast!

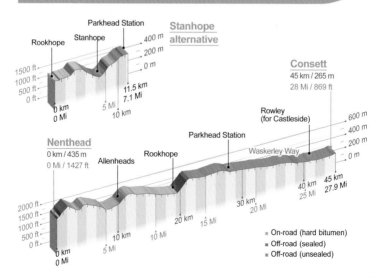

- On-road (hard bitumen)
- Off-road (sealed)
- Off-road (unsealed)

What to See & Do

• **Important note on mining landscape:** The moorland landscape from the Alston area to the Waskerley Way is littered with remains of old mine workings. These include shafts, adits (horizontal tunnels for drainage or access) and old buildings such as smelt mills. **These are often in a serious state of decay and should not be entered.** Also beware of 'hummocky' ground which often contains pit entrances. 'Beehive' cones of stones covered pit entrances and may have partly collapsed. Some of these underground workings were hundreds of feet deep.

• **Black Hill,** at the end of the steep climb out of Nenthead, is the **highest point on the C2C** (609 metres or 1998 feet, so at least your head will be above 2000 feet!). Naturally much photographed.

• Despite a working history as a lead mining centre **Allenheads** is an estate village with some fine architecture that has managed to reinvent itself as a small, popular tourist centre. Unlike lead mining in Nenthead the industry here was controlled by one aristocratic family, the Blackett-Beaumonts. Once a village of nearly 800 people it now has 200. The Allenheads mine closed in 1896, many workers emigrating to the colonies. The **Heritage Centre** explores the history of the local lead mines. An **Armstrong hydraulic engine** is another reminder of the village's past and one of the heritage centre's main attractions.

Cobbles and battlements at Stanhope

The Waskerley Way signals the start of easy, traffic-free riding

• Around tiny **Rookhope** is a wonderful collection of relics of the thriving mining industry that once dominated the area. You pass the remains of **Grove Rake fluospar mine**, active as late as 1999, and further down the valley is the **Lintzgarth Arch**, the only remains of a bridge that once carried a two mile long horizontal flue across the valley. This was cleaned by child labour to recoup lead deposits accumulated from smelting fumes.

• The off-road route heads over Stanhope Moor, following the line of an old railway, once the **highest standard gauge route in Britain**, that carried mineral ore to Consett (your route continuing there as the Waskerley Way). The remains of **Bolt's Law Engine House** have been well-maintained, despite being ruins and add further to the unique atmosphere of this fine moorland crossing. Look out for the fascinating explanation plaque.

• The southern route option goes via **Stanhope**, self-proclaimed capital of Weardale and attractive market town with attractions as varied as a fossilized tree and an open-air swimming pool. Durham Dales Centre is set in the lovely Castle Gardens, the castle really being an elaborate 18th century folly.

• The **Waskerley Way** boasts plenty of flora and fauna and the spectacular 175ft high **Hownsgill Viaduct** provides a grand finale on your approach to Consett.

Directions

1 Facing North Pennine Cycles in Nenthead going right will take you steeply up the A689 which is the road option. Take the first left after about 1km (0.6 miles) which will bring you to Black Hill - congratulations you've reached the highest point on the C2C.

For the very steep but slightly shorter off-road option to Black Hill face North Pennine Cycles and go to the right of the former reading room (now a community shop). Almost immediately split left up the cobbled lane. It becomes tarmac just behind the church. Jink ninety degrees left and take the right up a gravel track heading straight up the hill, eventually joining the road at Black Hill and here go left to rejoin the main route.

Having passed the sign for Northumberland navigation to Rookhope is now easy; about 1.25km (0.75 miles) after Black Hill turn right **2**, following signs for Allenheads village. Descending towards Allenheads ignore a couple of lefts to Spartylea and Thorn Green bunkhouse to cross the river and immediately turn right at the T-junction signed for Allenheads.

Through Allenheads centre pass the Allenheads Inn and the Hemmel Cafe and cross the B6295 to climb over the hill known as Currick **3**.

> *i* **Stanhope (Durham Dales)** Castle Gardens
> 01388 527650 www.durhamdalescentre.co.uk

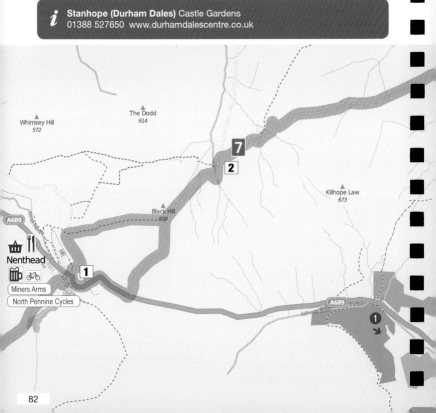

1 LOW CORNRIGGS FARM
Cowshill DL13 1AQ
01388 537600
www.cornriggsfarm.co.uk
Min 2 night stay unless in a group of 6+
Collection from Allenheads or Nenthead

2 THE ALLENHEADS INN
Allenheads NE47 9HJ
01434 685200
www.allenheadsinn.co.uk
Accommodation open Easter to November but
will open out of season for groups

3 OLD SCHOOL HOUSE
Allenheads NE47 9HR
01434 685040   www.acart.org.uk

4 BLACKETTS RETREAT
Newhouses Allenheads NE47 9HX
01434 685260 / 0794 0812634
www.allenheadsC2C.com

B THORN GREEN
Allenheads NE47 9JQ
01434 685234
www.thorngreenaccommodation.co.uk

B ALLENHEADS LODGE
Allenheads NE47 9HW
0191 515 5300
www.springboard-ne.org.uk

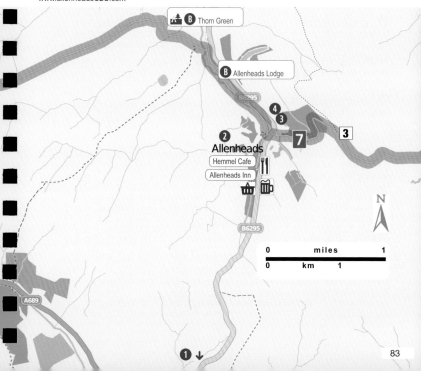

5 SWALLOWS REST
Redburn House Rookhope DL13 2DE
01388 517589 01325 788141
www.britishholidaysdirect.co.uk

6 THE ROOKHOPE INN
Rookhope DL13 2BG
01388 517215   www.rookhopeinn.co.uk

7 THE OLD VICARAGE
Stotsfield Burn Rookhope DL13 2AE
01388 517375

8 HORSLEY HALL
Eastgate DL13 2LJ
01388 517239   www.horsleyhall.co.uk

9 CROSS KEYS INN
Eastgate DL13 2HW
01388 517234 Mob 07881 553454
www.crosskeyseastgate.co.uk

B BARRINGTON BUNKHOUSE
Rookhope DL13 2BG   01388 517656
www.barrington-bunkhouse-rookhope.com

B FELL HOUSE COTTAGE BUNKHOUSE
Rookhope DL13 2BD
01388 517927 / 07909 443866
www.fellhousecottage.co.uk
Single night stay need min 6 people

B HOLE HOUSE BUNKHOUSE
Eastgate DL13 2HX
01388 517184

Ignore any minor turnings on this road and head into County Durham, soon freewheeling down a valley with Rookhope Burn on your right. Pass the old mine workings, the Linztgarth Arch ruins and a left to Blanchland **4** to come into Rookhope village.

The off-road route from Rookhope is the former railway track across Stanhope Moor, picked up by turning left just after the Rookhope Inn, marked as Hylton Terrace and signed for Waskerley **5**. At the first immediate split head right (not left to the river) and at the next split by the small stone structure go left. Soon, by an NCN milepost, you bear left again. After a steepish climb of just over a mile you pass the remains of Bolts Law Engine House and the gradient levels out, the wide stone track (some suspension or at least fat tyres advised) now providing magnificent sweeping views.

Just over 4km after joining the track in Rookhope a rougher, grassy track splits off to the right **6**. This is the official route, though the track at the time of writing was very rutted and quite tricky to ride unless you are used to off-roading and singletrack riding in particular. The well-made track continues ahead and a sign advises you not to cycle it as this may jeopardise negotiations with landowners. However, it doesn't seem there is anything to stop you pushing your bike the 300m or so to the minor road and turning right to avoid the rutted section (indeed the warning sign expressly says rights of walkers are not jeopardised).

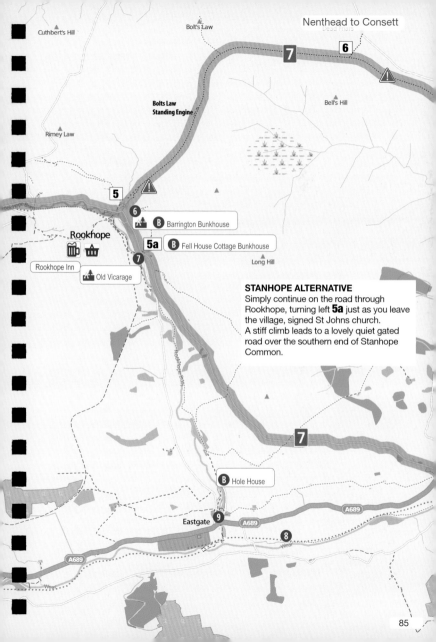

7

6

Cuthbert's Hill

Bolt's Law

Bolts Law
Standing Engine

Bell's Hill

Rimey Law

5

Rookhope Burn

6 **B** Barrington Bunkhouse

5a **B** Fell House Cottage Bunkhouse

Rookhope

Rookhope Inn

7

Long Hill

Old Vicarage

STANHOPE ALTERNATIVE

Simply continue on the road through
Rookhope, turning left **5a** just as you leave
the village, signed St Johns church.
A stiff climb leads to a lovely quiet gated
road over the southern end of Stanhope
Common.

7

B Hole House

Eastgate **9** A689

8

Wear

A689

Wear

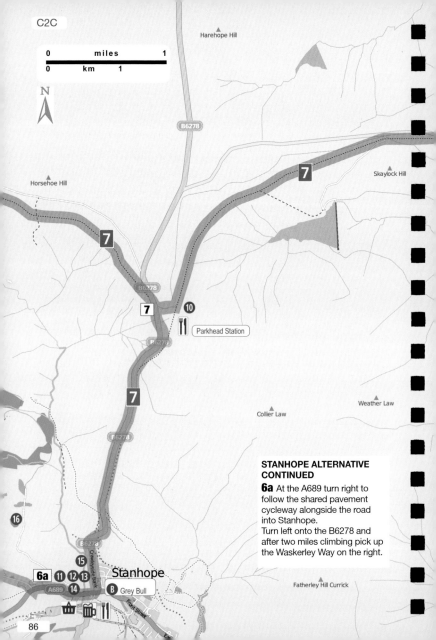

Harehope Hill

miles 1
km 1

N

B6278

Horsehoe Hill

Skaylock Hill

7

7

B6278

7 ⑩

Parkhead Station

B6278

Weather Law

7

Collier Law

B6278

STANHOPE ALTERNATIVE CONTINUED

6a At the A689 turn right to follow the shared pavement cycleway alongside the road into Stanhope.
Turn left onto the B6278 and after two miles climbing pick up the Waskerley Way on the right.

⑯

B6278

⑮

6a ⑪ ⑫ ⑬

Stanhope

A689 ⑭

B Grey Bull

Fatherley Hill Currick

Skaylock Hill

⑩ PARKHEAD STATION
Stanhope Moor DL13 2ES
01388 526434   www.parkheadstation.co.uk

⑪ BONNY MOORHEN
25 Front Street Stanhope DL13 2TS
01388 528214   0771 527 7300

⑫ PACKHORSE INN
8 Market Place Stanhope DL13 2UJ
 01388 528407   www.packhorsestanhope.co.uk

⑬ RED LODGE B&B
2 Market Place Stanhope DL13 2UN
01388 526 152 / 07429 521 914
redlodgebnb.com

⑭ BURNSIDE BRACE
23 Rose Terrace Stanhope DL13 2PE
01388 528727 www.burnsidebraceguesthouse.com

⑮ BANKFOOT
1 West Terrace Stanhope DL13 2PD
01388 528747 07570 454647
www.bankfootbandb.co.uk

⑯ BELLE VUE COUNTRY B&B
Hall Road, Stanhope DL13 2EZ
01388 526225   www.tranquil-life.info

Ⓑ GREY BULL BUNKHOUSE
17 West Terrace Stanhope
01388 529428 / 07885 676575

7 Meet the B6278 and jink right then left across it, up a track to pass Parkhead Station B&B and cafe. Bear left to follow the Waskerley Way and into open moorland again. The Waskerley Reservoir appears down to your right.

STANHOPE ALTERNATIVE
Descend to meet the A689 and head left **6a**, using the pavement cycle lane. Just under 1 km (0.6 miles) after turning onto the pavement cycle lane alongside the A689 turn left, just before the Grey Bull pub and bunkhouse, up the B6278 (town centre is straight ahead). This turns into a very steep climb. 4 km after joining the B road you see the track turning to Parkhead Station on the right and rejoin the main route **7**.

 No rail stations en route but if you need 'bail out' options towards the end of the route Broomhaugh is about 17km (10.5 miles) north of Castleside up the A68, with regular trains to Newcastle, and Bishop Auckland is around 26km (16 miles) south-east of Stanhope. The latter branch line links to the east coast main line at Darlington.

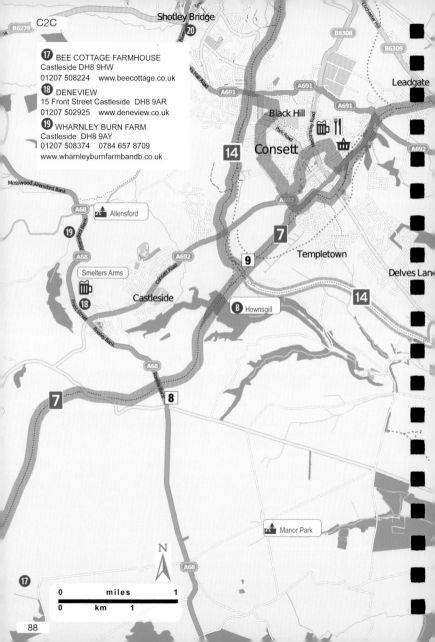

C2C

⑳ CROWN & CROSSED SWORDS HOTEL
Front Street Shotley Bridge DH8 0HU
01207 502006   crownandcrossedswords.co.uk

Ⓑ HOWNSGILL BUNKHOUSE
Hownsgill Farm Consett DH8 9AA
01207 503597   07904 050120
www.c2cstopoff.co.uk

Ⓑ CONSETT YMCA
Parliament Street Consett DH8 5DH
01207 502680 www.consettymca.com
Groups preferred

MANOR PARK CARAVAN PARK
Broadmeadows, Rippon Burn, Castleside DH8 9HD
01207 501000

ALLENSFORD CARAVAN PARK
Pemberton Road, Castleside DH8 9BA
01207 593624
www.allensfordcaravanpark.co.uk

The well made unsealed track takes you past picnic sites and across a track crossroads and through a car park to cross the main A68 in Rowley **8** (Castleside is just over 1km / 0.6 miles to the left). Pass over the very impressive Hownsgill Viaduct just before coming to Lydgett's Junction marked by a large smelt wagon **9**. Carry straight on to finish at Sunderland or split off left, passing behind the car park, to finish at Newcastle. Ignore signs for Lanchester Valley to the right.

Consett

The C2C end; Roker Pier seen through the Star Map sculpture

Consett ~ Sunderland

For most of the way the Consett and Sunderland railway path is flat and easy to follow. The landscape presents a strong contrast; the Wear Valley is delightfully green and wooded in places, dotted with specially commissioned sculptures and other monuments, whilst Sunderland presents a grand post-industrial spectacle that is steadily and thoughtfully being regenerated and makes the most of its fine mix of museums and architecture.

Despite many of the settlements along the way clearly still suffering some deprivation after the loss of much heavy industry, there is plenty of interest and excitement on and near the trail. Foremost in terms of visitor numbers is probably Beamish Open Air Museum though the Washington Wildfowl Wetlands Centre is in fact internationally important as well as being fascinating.

As you head downstream there are some fine views across the Wear and all the while you are accompanied by a brilliantly varied mix of trailside sculptures that have become synonymous with the trail itself.

Route Info

Distance 39 km (24 miles)

Off - road 39 km (24 miles)   The trail is increasingly tarmac, though a few stone and cinder sections remain. Once, real difficulties in navigation lay in negotiating Sunderland city centre but a 'north bank' route has been introduced and is a great improvement in terms of track condition and ease of navigation. There are also plenty of mileposts to help navigation, perhaps the only downside being more access barriers than the Newcastle option along the Derwent Walk.

Terrain Physically this is the easiest section of the whole route, being virtually all downhill. The tendency is to speed on but doing this you can easily miss the many attractions close to the route.

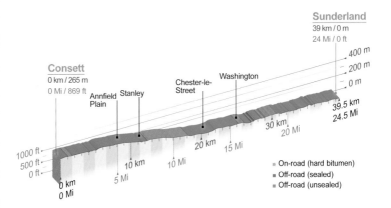

On-road (hard bitumen)
Off-road (sealed)
Off-road (unsealed)

What to See & Do

• Of the many specially commissioned sculptures along the C2C route **Terris Novalis** is one of the most outstanding. 20 feet high stainless steel surveying instruments symbolise the regeneration of Consett after the closure of the massive steel works that was once the heart of the area. Other artworks include **Transformers**, just after Leadgate, and **King Coal** on your approach to Chester-le-Street.

• **Beamish Open Air Museum** is one of the North's premier museums with full-scale recreations of the past industrial and agricultural life of the North-East. Visit a drift mine, pit cottages, a 19th century manor farm or hop on a tram, plus lots more at this huge site in Beamish Burn.

• **Causey Arch**, centrepiece of a beautiful picnic site, is one of the main features of the **Tanfield Railway** and is the oldest surviving single-arch railway bridge in the world. The railway was opened in 1725 and used horses to haul small coal wagons along wooden tracks. It is now a steam railway run by volunteers. Open on selected days.

• Few physical remains are left of the Roman influence on **Chester-le-Street** but it boasts an impressive church spire and effigies of the Lumley family inside. The most remarkable church feature though is the **Ankers House Museum**; see how an Anchorite lived, walled up for life to pray.

Passing the unmissable Terris Novalis

Popular trail section near Washington

• **Washington** was created as a new town in 1967, designed to attract industry and jobs to a declining area. Divided into self-contained village type settlements and with planned segregation of cars and pedestrians. **'F' Pit Mining Museum** on Albany Way has a winding house and engine on display. The **Arts Centre Washington**, Fatfield, houses exhibitions and performances.

• **Washington Wildfowl Trust** is an important and extensive site for wildlife, especially winter wildfowl and is a great C2C cafe stop (no need to pay to enter the full site; just lock your bike outside and enjoy the cafe's lovely vantage point over the reserve. **Washington Old Hall** in District 4, Washington Village is

National Trust property incorporating the remains of the home of George Washington's ancestors within a 17th century manor house.

• **James Steel Park** surrounds the Wear between Fatfield and Barmston and houses **Victoria Viaduct** (completed on Victoria's coronation day, 28th June, 1838) and **Worm Hill** of Lambton Worm fame. The 'Worm' was a mythical dragon that brought about a family curse when slain. **The Penshaw Monument** is based on the Temple of Hephaestus in Athens. A memorial to 'Radical Jack' Lambton, 1st Earl of Durham, it was built in 1844 from public subscription. Good views of it from James Steel Park and around Cox Green.

Wearmouth road and rail bridges

• **Fulwell Mill** North-west of Roker is the most complete windmill in the north east and fully restored.

• **Hylton Castle's** 15th century gatehouse still survives. The west side has impressive battlements.

• **North East Land, Sea & Air Museums** 1.5 miles north of the C2C in North Hylton, has aircraft and military vehicles.

• **Monkwearmouth Station Museum** is housed behind the train station's grand classical facade. This railway museum has a genuine 19th century atmosphere with a Victorian booking office, Victorian and Edwardian cycle displays and lots more.

• **Sunderland Museum & Winter Gardens** give you the lowdown on the town's history alongside a fine art gallery plus over 1,500 plants and flowers.

• **Northern Gallery for Contemporary Art** is the north-east's premier collection of contemporary art.

• **Sunderland Volunteer Life Brigade Museum**. Near the end of the C2C. Volunteers preceded the RNLI as the main body responsible on this stretch of coast for ship rescue. The Brigade is now separated from the coastguard service and acts as an auxiliary service for coastal services and cliff rescue. Still a working brigade, it's only one of 3 left out of an original 40.

- **Sunderland** was once one of the world's greatest shipbuilding towns. The shipbuilding area can still be seen from Wearmouth Bridge. It's now one of England's newest cities.
- **The area around** St. Peter's Riverside houses the **National Glass Centre** which has galleries, a shop and a restaurant. **St.Peter's Church**, nearby, is one of Northumbria's oldest churches. Home of the Venerable Bede, 'Father of English History'.

- **Wearmouth** also houses the **Stadium of Light** football ground and the C2C passes a **new marina** development. **Wearmouth Bridge** road bridge dwarfs the railway bridge next to it. Built 1927-8, the parapet has a medallion showing the 1796 bridge it replaced. A technological wonder of its day.
- **St. Andrew's Church**, Roker is regarded as the 'cathedral' of William Morris' Arts and Craft Movement.

Easy riding into Sunderland

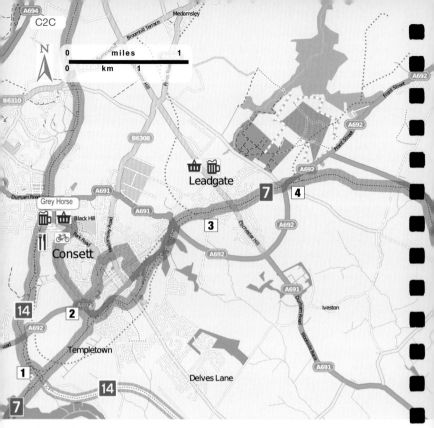

Directions

1 Lydgett's Junction is marked by the unmistakable bulk of the Smelt Wagon, in effect a routes crossroads. Those heading directly for Newcastle / Tynemouth (NCN 14) should bear left, simply marked as a narrow track. For Sunderland (NCN 72) and / or Consett centre go straight on (ignore a right to Lanchester and Durham on NCN14).

Just after Terris Novalis sculpture you can choose the Consett centre option to the left **2** or carry straight on to parallel the south side of the A692 on shared use pathway, briefly leaving the main road to cross Delves Lane.

Between Consett and Washington it's mainly a matter of following the railpath. Coming into Leadgate very briefly jink left then right onto South Cross Street **3** and pick up the railpath again.

East of Leadgate head across the A692 roundabout and into the squiggles of the maze earthworks **4** and onto a lovely open stretch of path with a lovely tarmac surface, riding beneath the highly impressive Transformers sculptures.

Approaching Annfield Plain the route becomes a little fiddlier; past a small fishing pond it jinks left then right over a road (Greencroft Parkway) **5** and on to cross the A693 on a

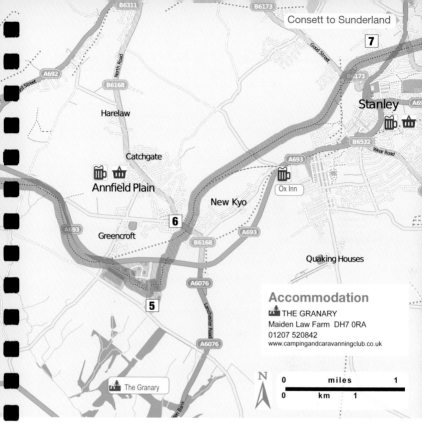

7

Stanley

Harelaw

Catchgate

Annfield Plain

New Kyo

Ox Inn

6

Greencroft

Quaking Houses

5

Accommodation

THE GRANARY
Maiden Law Farm DH7 0RA
01207 520842
www.campingandcaravanningclub.co.uk

| 0 | miles | 1 |

| 0 | km | 1 |

 The Granary

bridge. Head down Dodds Terrace then St Aidans Terrace and jink left through a wall to meet the main road in Annfield Plain by the Tescos superstore **6**. Straight across here, picking up the railpath down the side of Spring Close, leading into open countryside. You pass north of Stanley centre on this traffic-free trail, where you see the distinctive 'tower and spire' church peaking above the rooftops over to your right, and cross the impressive iron bridges **7**.

Sunderland only has trains from two mainline operators running through it: Grand Central operate a direct Sunderland-London service which carries bikes. The line to London also stops at several stations in the north of England north of and including York. Spaces are non reservable.
Northern services give local connections. For their cycle carriage details see page 22.
To connect with other rail operators' services (e.g. ScotRail) you will need to change at Newcastle (see page 116).

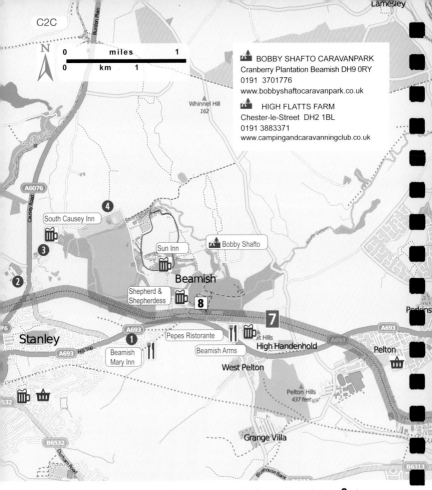

BOBBY SHAFTO CARAVANPARK
Cranberry Plantation Beamish DH9 0RY
0191 3701776
www.bobbyshaftocaravanpark.co.uk

HIGH FLATTS FARM
Chester-le-Street DH2 1BL
0191 3883371
www.campingandcaravanningclub.co.uk

Through a lovely stretch of woodland you come to the iron cows sculptures **8** where Beamish is signed as just 200m off the trail. Through more open country your approach to Chester-le-Street is marked by another well-known C2C sculpture, King Coal **9**. Cross the rail line (the Angel of the North is visible from here on a good day). Soon you come to the easiest route to navigate if visiting Chester-le-Street (despite not being the shortest); head off the trail onto the A167 (actually signed as NCN 725 from the trail itself, to both Durham and Chester-le-Street). There are cycle lanes for much of the way as you descend across the A693 to reach a mini-roundabout where the town centre is straight ahead.
Back on the main C2C head under the M1 and over the A182 **10**.

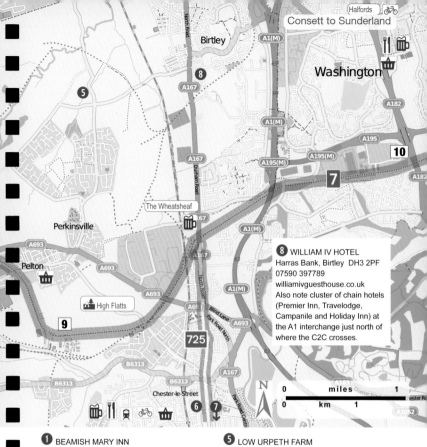

8 WILLIAM IV HOTEL
Harras Bank, Birtley DH3 2PF
07590 397789
williamivguesthouse.co.uk
Also note cluster of chain hotels
(Premier Inn, Travelodge,
Campanile and Holiday Inn) at
the A1 interchange just north of
where the C2C crosses.

1 BEAMISH MARY INN
No Place Beamish DH9 0AQ
0191 3700237
www.beamishmaryinn.com

2 THE BALL ALLEY BED AND BREAKFAST
Shield Row Stanley DH9 0LH
01207 281577 / 07528 233253 www.ballalley.co.uk

3 SOUTH CAUSEY INN
Beamish Burn Road Stanley DH9 0LS
01207 235555 www.southcausey.co.uk

4 BEST WESTERN BEAMISH HALL
Beamish DH9 0YB
01207 233733 www.beamish-hall.co.uk

5 LOW URPETH FARM
Ouston Chester-le-Street DH2 1BD
0191 4102901 www.lowurpeth.co.uk

6 LAMBTON ARMS HOTEL
Front Street
Chester-le-Street DH3 3BJ
0191 3883265 www.wearinns.co.uk

7 HOLLYCROFT B&B
11 The Parade Chester-le-Street DH3 3LR
0191 3887088 www.staydurham.co.uk

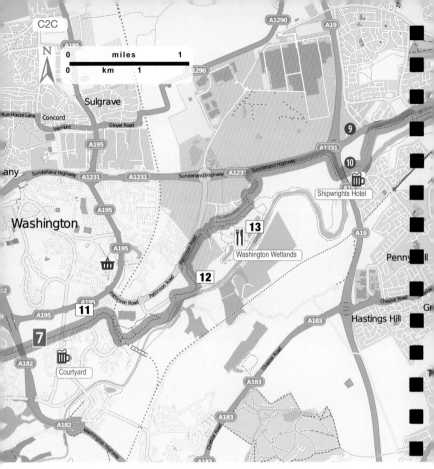

Head across Newman Lane **11** and bear right down a tree-lined track by a railway on the left to come into James Steel Park.

Bear left to pass under railway bridge into James Steel Park and swing right to descend steeply to River Wear. By green footbridge climb away from river onto a series of paths **12**. Turn right parallel to a nondescript road (Pattinson Road) and right at the next roundabout and almost immediately left onto a tarmac path, soon coming to Washington Wildfowl Wetlands - a great cafe stop where you can sit and watch the wildlife at the same time **13**.

The track passes through woods, bearing left at a tarmac road then right in about 150m to come alongside the very major A1231 on your left with fine views across to the Penshaw monument. This track swings right and takes you under the A19 to a steep descent to the Shipwrights Hotel.

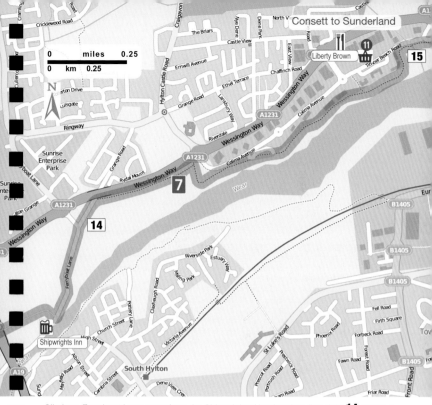

Climb up Ferryboat Lane away from the Shipwrights Hotel and go first right **14**, bearing right off the road just before the A1231 bridge crosses ahead of you, picking up the excellent traffic-free trail. The trail climbs to briefly run alongside the A1231 before disappearing back down towards the river.

It brushes an office development on Timber Beach Road **15** and again disappears down towards the river.

9 PREMIER INN
Wessington Way Castletown SR5 3HR
0871 5279058
www.premierinn.com

10 SHIPWRIGHTS HOTEL Ferryboat Lane
North Hylton SR5 3HW
0191 5495139

11 PREMIER INN
Timber Beach Road Castletown SR5 3XG
0871 5279056

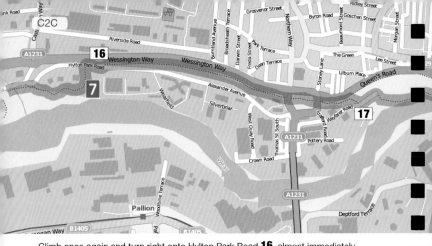

Climb once again and turn right onto Hylton Park Road **16**, almost immediately bearing left onto a fine traffic-free trail. Shortly after passing under a large trunk road interchange the best route option heads off down to the right, bearing left onto and right off Wayfarer Road **17**.

There's now a fine stretch of riding alongside the Wear until meeting the impressive Wearmouth road and rail bridges **18** (Sunderland centre is across the road bridge here). A landslip in 2013 meant a slight detour behind St. Peter's Metro station and over the main road, dropping down to the right onto Bonners Field and at the bottom squiggling through an access control and bearing left for the final easy and rather splendid section, alongside the Wear **19**, onto Sand Point Road **20**, round the Marina and along the seafront at Roker. The route's official end is at the fine Star Map sculpture, built so it frames the lighthouse.

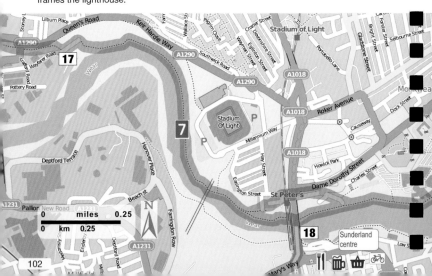

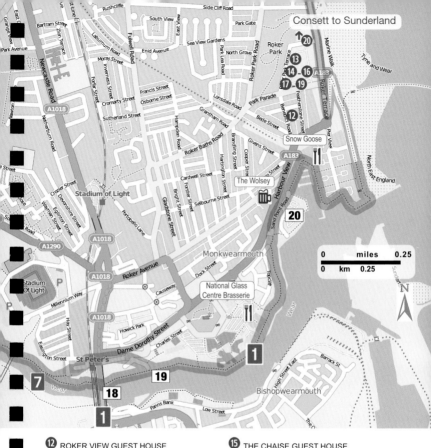

Consett to Sunderland

12 ROKER VIEW GUEST HOUSE
2 Benedict Road Roker SR6 0NX
0191 5657354 0780 1089240
www.sunderlandguesthouse.co.uk

13 BEST WESTERN ROKER HOTEL
Roker Terrace Roker SR6 9ND
08445 767676
www.bestwestern.co.uk
Possible weekend min stay conditions

14 BALMORAL & TERRACE GUEST HOUSES
2/3 Roker Terrace Roker SR6 9NB
0191 565 9217 / 5650132
www.balmoralandterrace.co.uk

15 THE CHAISE GUEST HOUSE
5 Roker Terrace Roker SR6 9NB
0191 5659218
www.thechaiseguesthouse.com

16 ABBEY GUESTHOUSE
17 Roker Terrace Roker SR6 9NB
0191 5140678
www.abbeygh.co.uk

See overleaf for further entries.

17 ASHBORNE GUEST HOUSE
7 St. George's Terrace Roker SR6 9LX
0191 5653997
www.ashborne-guesthouse.co.uk

18 ABINGDON GUEST HOUSE
5 St George's Terrace Roker SR6 9LX
0191 5140689 07543 123381
www.abingdonguesthouse.co.uk

19 APRIL GUEST HOUSE
12 St. George's Terrace Roker SR6 9LX
0191 5659550   www.aprilguesthouse.co.uk

20 LEMONFIELD GUEST HOUSE
Sea Lane Seaburn SR6 8EE
0191 5293018
www.lemonfieldhotel.com

Winter Gardens Sunderland

i **Sunderland** Customer Service Centre, 31-32 Fawcett Street 0191 5205550
www.sunderland.gov.uk

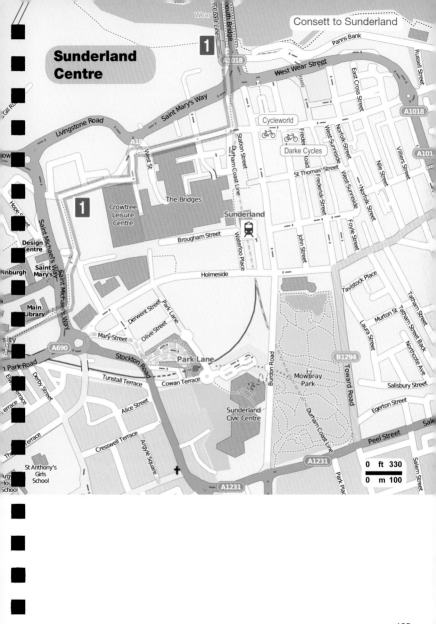

Sunderland Centre

105

*Tynemouth Long Sands
provide a magnificent
finale to the route*

Consett ~ Tynemouth

Almost immediately out of Consett and Shotley Bridge it's clear you have left the heather moorland behind you and are in gentler surroundings as you head down the Derwent Walk, along a former railway through idyllic woodland and pasture. Ebchester has a Roman history and an attractive conservation area at its heart, whilst Gibside boasts the magnificent National Trust estate, worth allowing some time out for.

Your major route decision comes where the river Derwent meets the Tyne; follow the southern bank along the Keelman's Way or the northern bank along Hadrian's Cycleway. Both are attractive routes, Keelman's Way having the more elevated views of the river and Hadrian's Cycleway having more in terms of visitor attractions, including Segedunum (a Roman fort museum at Wallsend) and a couple of lovely marinas at St Peter's and Royal Quays.

Be aware though that the Tyne cycle tunnel, used to hop from south bank to north bank, is closed until August 2014 (and possibly beyond this), though there is a cycle-carrying replacement shuttle bus service. The final run in along the Tyne estuary to Tynemouth is amongst the most memorable sections of the whole C2C and Tynemouth itself is a splendid town. Probably its chief asset is the lovely sweep of beach aptly named Longsands backed by the equally aptly named splendours of the Grand Hotel.

Route Info

Distance Tyne North Bank: 46 km (28.5 miles)
Tyne South Bank: 47.5 km (29.5 miles)

Off-road Tyne North Bank: 40.5 km (25 miles) Tyne South Bank: 38.5 km (24 miles). Lengthy sections on well-surfaced off-road track on various designated trails. The Derwent Walk is followed for much of its length from Consett to Swalwell and is a pleasure to ride with very few restrictive access barriers. The route along the Tyne's north bank (Hadrian's Cycleway) is greatly improved from the original C2C route with a lot of new traffic-free trail. The alternative option along the Tyne's southern bank has also been much improved. Indeed it's a testament to the work that Sustrans have done locally that your wheels are on traffic-free tarmac for the majority of the ride into Newcastle, whichever option you take.

Terrain Generally gentle downhill or on the level pedalling.

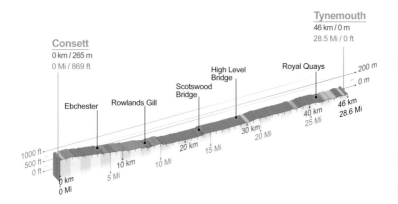

Consett
0 km / 265 m
0 Mi / 869 ft

Tynemouth
46 km / 0 m
28.5 Mi / 0 ft

Ebchester
Rowlands Gill
Scotswood Bridge
High Level Bridge
Royal Quays

Keelman's Way option

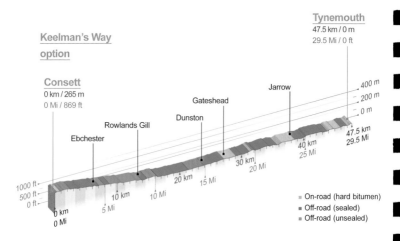

Consett
0 km / 265 m
0 Mi / 869 ft

Tynemouth
47.5 km / 0 m
29.5 Mi / 0 ft

Ebchester
Rowlands Gill
Dunston
Gateshead
Jarrow

- On-road (hard bitumen)
- Off-road (sealed)
- Off-road (unsealed)

CYCLISTS
SLOW DOWN
& GIVE WAY

Cullercoats 1¼
Whitley Bay 2½
St Mary's Island 4½

Tynemouth's elegant Front Street is lined
with pubs, cafes and restaurants

What to See & Do

• Skirting Consett you are passing through part of a 700 acre site of the former Consett steelworks, closed in 1980, once employing many thousands. Much of the subsequent section follows the lovely **Derwent Walk Path**, based on the line of the 19th century Derwent Valley Railway. It crosses spectacular viaducts such as Pontburn, Fogoesburn and Nine Arches. Now tree-clad along much of its length, it houses wildlife such as woodpeckers, sparrowhawks and most spectacularly red kites. The largest area of ancient woodland is around Thornley Woodland Centre. **Derwent Walk Country Park** surrounding the path is one of the largest in northern England.

• **Shotley Bridge**, once the home of 17th century swordmakers, still houses reminders of its spa town origins, such as the Cutlers Hall.

• **Ebchester** is the site of the Roman fort Vindamora and has a small cluster of ancient buildings at its heart. Small museum at Mains Farm includes hypocaust (heated space under the floor of a Roman house). The site was once on Dere Street, the Roman road bringing supplies north to the Firth of Forth.

• **Rowlands Gill,** developed as a mining settlement, is now a pleasant suburb. The nearby National Trust **Gibside** estate has beautiful 18th century landscaped grounds including Old Hall, an extraordinary Palladian Chapel, Orangery, British Liberty statue and Banqueting Hall. Allow a couple of hours to stroll round grounds. Coal-owner George Bowes was responsible for most of the magnificent relandscaping and is buried in the chapel crypt.

Speeding downhill on the Derwent Walk

Riding on the Gateshead Millennium bridge with the Baltic landmark in the background

• **Newcastle-upon-Tyne** is most famous for heavy industry and coal. Previously it was one of the largest ship building and repair centres in the world and had one of the most elegant townscapes in the country and countless interesting buildings and monuments remain despite modernisation.

• The city is also famous for bridges, most notably the **Gateshead Millennium Bridge**. The world's only tilting bridge, allowing shipping to pass underneath and highlighted by a spectacular high-tech light show in the evening. It's also a fantastic traffic-free link for cyclists (and pedestrians), allowing you to switch quickly between Hadrian's Cycleway on the Tyne's north bank and the Keelman's Way on the south bank. Other bridges near city centre make

for a spectacular riverscape from west to east: **Redheugh Road Bridge**, **King Edward Railway Bridge**, **Queen Elizabeth II Metro Bridge**, **High Level Bridge** (railway, road and cycle / foot passengers. Designed by Robert Stephenson and one of the wonders of the Railway Age), **Hydraulic Swing Bridge** (one of the first large opening bridges in the world), **Tyne Road Bridge** (1928), suspended by the huge suspension arch, symbol of Newcastle and last but not least is the Gateshead Millennium Bridge.

• Two unique riverside landmarks are the silvery glass curves of **The Sage** music venue and the **BALTIC Centre for Contemporary Art,** housed in a former flour mill with rooftop viewing gallery.

- **Newcastle's centre** boasts a wealth of attractions. The **Quayside** area is famous for its Sunday morning market. Nearby is **Bessie Surtees' House**, a 17th century timber-framed building.
- **Grey Street** has been described as one of the most elegant streets in Europe and culminates in the magnificent Grey's Monument, built to celebrate the role of the eponymous politician in the 1832 Reform Act which was passed during Earl Grey's premiership
- **Castle Keep** is part of the castle built between 1172 and 1178 by Henry II. The original castle gave its name to the city. **Black Gate** was added to the castle in 1247. Passing through the gate look out for the Heron Pit, an underground prison.
- **St Nicholas' Cathedral** has a remarkably beautiful 15th century 'crown' spire. The only other in the UK in this style is in Edinburgh. Inside are the Collingwood Monument and the brass lectern.
- Just west of Central station is the **Centre for Life** housing the **Life Science Museum** where DNA, genetics, the human body and much more are presented in a fun and educational way.
- **Discovery Museum** Over £12 million has been spent here. The displays on the Tyne's history should be well worth a look.
- The **city walls** were built during the reigns of Edward I and Edward II and several sections still remain.

© Creative Commons ppz

Grey's Monument, Newcastle centre

St Peters Marina seen from the C2C

• The Tyne Estuary gradually opens out as you near journey's end. Here the route runs above the snugly tucked away St Peter's Marina, with its beautifully restored fishing boats, before going past **Segedunum Roman Fort Museum** marking the eastern terminus of Hadrian's Wall.

• **Royal Quays** is an enormous shopping and housing redevelopment area. Look out for the viewpoint in Redburn Dene park. **Wet'n'Wild** at Royal Quays is a 'chutes and waves' swimming pool.

• Passing through the quayside area of **North Shields** the two white towers above and on the quay are navigational aids that ships could use to navigate a safe passage up the Tyne (done by aligning them). **Clifford's Fort** near the Fish Quay is the remains of a seventeenth century armed fort named after Lord Clifford of Cabal.

• **Black Middens** are the notorious rocks near the Tyne entrance that claimed 5 ships in 3 days in November 1864.

• The **Collingwood Monument** is named after the Newcastle native who took command of the fleet at Trafalgar after Nelson's death.

• **Tynemouth Priory and Castle** is surrounded by curiously eroded gravestones. An 11th century Norman church that developed within a castle enclosure.

• If you choose the Keelman's Way along the Tyne's southern bank you will pass near **Jarrow Hall, Anglo Saxon Farm, Village and Bede Museum** in Jarrow, just east of the Tyne foot and cycle tunnel which lets you swap from the Keelman's Way to Hadrian's Cycleway on the north bank (see pages 126-127). The museum is based on the famous medieval monk's abode.

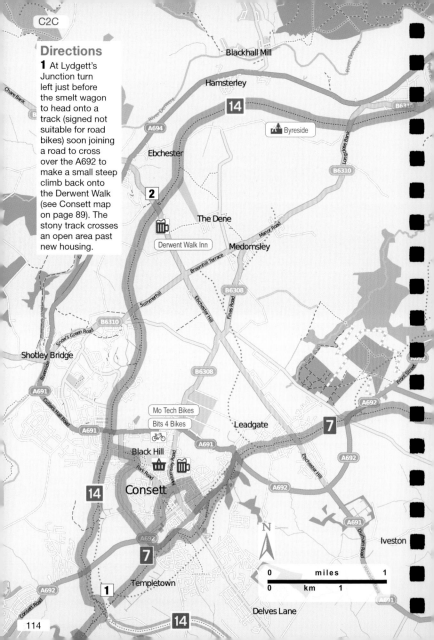

Directions

1 At Lydgett's Junction turn left just before the smelt wagon to head onto a track (signed not suitable for road bikes) soon joining a road to cross over the A692 to make a small steep climb back onto the Derwent Walk (see Consett map on page 89). The stony track crosses an open area past new housing.

Blackhall Mill

Hamsterley

14

River Derwent

A694

🏰 Byreside

Ebchester

Longhidge Bank

B6310

2

🍺

The Dene

Derwent Walk Inn

Manor Road

Medomsley

Broomhill Terrace

B6308

Summerhill

Ebchester Hill

Fines Road

B6310

Snow's Green Road

B6308

Shotley Bridge

Riverside

A691

Cutlers Hall Road

A691

Mo Tech Bikes

Bits 4 Bikes

🚲

Leadgate

7

A692

Ebchester Hill

A692

Black Hill

🛒

Park Road

Medomsley Road

🍺

A691

14

Consett

A692

A692

A691

Durham Road

Iveston

7

N

1

Templetown

Consett Road

A692

Delves Lane

14

| 0 | | miles | | 1 |
| 0 | | km | | 1 |

Accommodation

🏕 BYRESIDE CARAVAN SITE
Hamsterley NE17 7RT
01207 560280
www.byresidecaravansite.co.uk

🏕 CUT THORN FARM
Fellside Rd nr Burnopfield NE16 6AA
01207 270230
www.campingandcaravanningclub.co.uk
www.gibsideyurts.co.uk

🏕 DERWENT CARAVAN PARK
Rowlands Gill NE39 1LG
01207 543383 derwentcaravanpark.wordpress.com

The route now passes through Blackhill and skirts Shotley Bridge; keep to tarmac paths well-signed as NCN 14 and soon you cross a main road and pass Blackhill cemetery then split off right onto the Derwent Walk traffic-free trail proper.

2 After nearly 6 km / 4 miles from the Lydgett's Junction pass under the B6309 (car park for Derwent Walk Inn on your left and pub just above you on the road).

Pass over a series of viaducts on the Derwent Walk and come to a minor road in Rowlands Gill **3** where the Derwent Walk runs into the Keelman's Way. Here go right then left onto B6314 pavement cycle lane. At the A694 keep right on the pavement cycle and right turn back onto the Derwent Walk.

4 Just over Nine Arches Viaduct the route leaves the Derwent Walk bearing left into Derwenthaugh Park (the Derwent Walk carries straight on to Swalwell). It descends to the river then crosses a stone bridge to pick up the river's north bank.

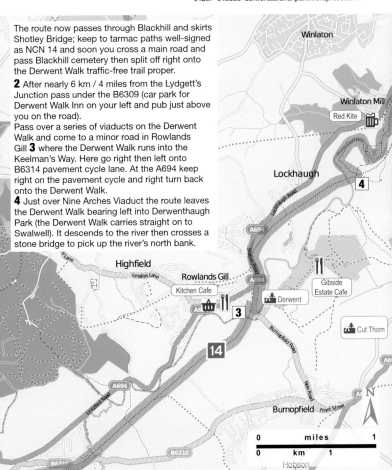

Journey's end, Tynemouth, does not have a main line rail connection and the local Metro trains back to Newcastle Central only accept folding bikes, so you may find yourself retracing the last 20 km (12.5 miles) or so of the route back to Newcastle.

Newcastle Central station is on the East Coast main line with direct trains south to London. If you are heading back to Whitehaven or Workington there are occasional direct trains though most change at Carlisle. Both the Cumbrian coast and the capital are about a three hour ride from Newcastle.

Cycle carriage:

Local Metro services take folding bikes only.

Newcastle-Carlisle trains may be either ScotRail or Northern Rail. **ScotRail's policy** is free bike carriage, subject to space, with cycle reservations needed in some cases (call 0344 811 0141) to check if one is required for your particular journey). Cycle reservations can be made online or as part of the ticket purchase at a station.
Northern's quoted policy is 'Bikes are carried free of charge at any time and you don't need to make reservations. The cycle space on trains is clearly marked, both internally and externally. Space is allocated on a first come, first served basis. We can only carry a maximum of two bikes per train but conductors have responsibility for the safety of their train and have the right to refuse entry if the train is busy.'

Most intercity services stopping at Newcastle are run by one of the following:
Virgin Trains East Coast - Cycle carriage free of charge subject to space. Two spaces to be reserved for tandems. Reservations essential and can be booked online.
Cross Country - Reservation strongly advised (call 0844 811 0124). All trains have two reservable bike spaces and one further space for unreserved bikes. Bikes for which no reservation has been made will be accepted on a first come, first served basis, subject to space being available.
Trans Pennine Express - Cycle carriage is free. Reservations advised (0345 600 1671 option 4). Reservations recommended at least 24 hours before departure.

The Keelman's Way heads over the rail bridge, the north bank route under it (see point **5** on the map)

Follow the traffic-free route north of the Derwent, under several roads (including the A1), to arrive at the meccano-like railway bridge **5**, just before the Derwent flows into the Tyne, and pass under it for the north bank route (NCN72); if you want the south bank route (NCN14) head over the footbridge next to the railway to cross the Derwent. See Keelman's Way route option overleaf.

If heading for the north bank and Hadrian's Cycleway bear left once under the railbridge and climb to join the cycle lanes over the Scotswood road bridge **6** over the Tyne.

1 EAST BYERMOOR GUEST HOUSE
Fellside Road Whickham NE16 5BD
01207 272687
www.eastbyermoor.co.uk

2 GIBSIDE HOTEL
Front Street Whickham NE16 4JG
0191 4889292
www.gibside-hotel.co.uk

3 PREMIER INN METRO CENTRE
Derwent Haugh Road Swalwell NE16 3BL
0871 527 8792
www.premierinn.com

4 HOLIDAY INN METRO CENTRE
Clasper Way, Swallwell NE16 3BE
01207 541100 / 0871 4234896
www. ihg.com

5 TRAVELODGE
Clasper Way Swalwell NE16 3BE
0871 984 6283
www.travelodge.co.uk

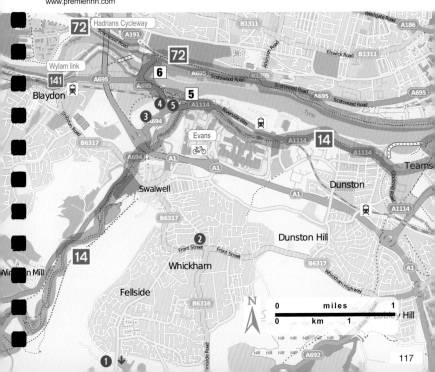

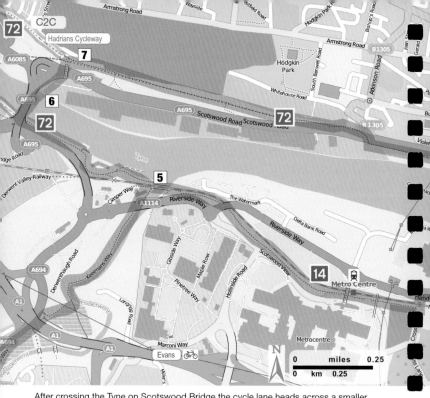

After crossing the Tyne on Scotswood Bridge the cycle lane heads across a smaller bridge to a T-junction with Hadrian's Cycleway where you bear right **7**. It's now simply a matter of following the signs along a very lengthy traffic-free section as you drop down alongside the A695 and use the Toucan to cross it. The cycle path then leaves the main road altogether and runs alongside the Tyne **8**.

> *i* **South Shields** Visitor Information Centre
> The Word, National Centre for the Written Word
> 45 Market Place, South Shields NE33 1JF 0191 427 1818
> theworduk.org

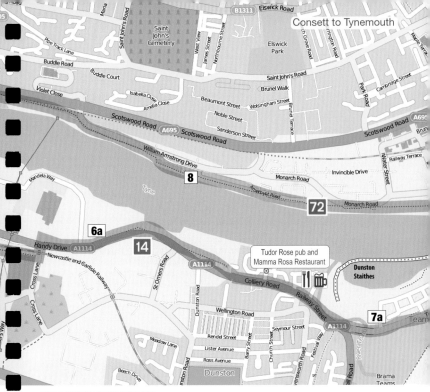

Tudor Rose pub and
Mamma Rosa Restaurant

KEELMAN'S WAY OPTION

5 Once over the rail bridge NCN 14 is pretty well signed; it takes you right past the giant shopping complex that is the Metro Centre before heading left under the railway and across a main road to bear right across Mandela Way **6a** .

The pavement cycle lane through Dunston peels away left off the A1114 to join Team Street and head across the river Team **7a**.

A quiet traffic-free section near Scotswood Bridge

6 COPTHORNE HOTEL
The Close Quayside NE1 3RT
0191 222 0333
www.millenniumhotels.co.uk

7 WATERSIDE HOTEL
48-52 Sandhill Quayside NE1 3JF
0755 2350296
www.waterside-hotel-newcastle.com

8 PREMIER INN
Quayside Lombard St NE1 3AE
0871 527 8804
www.premierinn.com

9 TRAVELODGE
Forster Street NE1 2NH
0871 9846164
www.travelodge.co.uk

H EUROHOSTEL NEWCASTLE
17 Carliol Square NE1 6UQ
0845 4900371
www.eurohostels.co.uk
Possible min stay requirements at weekends

H ALBATROSS BACKPACKERS IN!
51 Grainger Street NE1 5JE
0191 2331330
albatrossnewcastle.co.uk

GREAT NORTH CYCLEWAY - NEWCASTLE CENTRE LINK AND FUTURE ROUTES

National Cycle Network Route 725, the Great North Cycleway, provides a handy link from the Tyne Bridge which the C2C passes under, to the heart of Newcastle.
The whole route is slated for completion by 2015 but some sections are already signed and in place, including Tyne Bridge to Gateshead Town Centre and on to Birtley via A167 and passing the Angel of the North at Eighton. There is also a small section in place near Chester-le-Street.

Gateshead Millennium Bridge

Gateshead Millennium Bridge

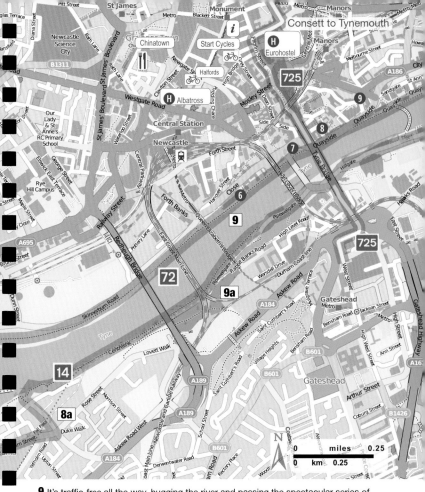

9 It's traffic-free all the way, hugging the river and passing the spectacular series of bridges spanning the Tyne between Newcastle and Gateshead. Be considerate of pedestrians here though as it's a magnet for locals and tourists alike.

KEELMAN'S WAY OPTION

8a Head left down Autumn Drive to the river by the incredible hulking mass of Dunston coal staithes. Head right on the riverside path.

9a The path joins the road at Pipewellgate on its approach to the cluster of bridges in Newcastle's centre. Past the lovely little swing bridge climb and turn left to pass underneath the massive glass curves of the Sage arts centre. The route now stays on the road past Gateshead Millennium Bridge.

10 JURYS INN
South Shore Road NE8 3AE
0191 401 6800
www.jurysinns.com

Note: Only accommodation providers near the
route in Newcastle and Gateshead are listed.
There is a plethora of similar opportunities
between the river and Newcastle town centre.
There are several good quality offerings around
Newcastle Central station.

The traffic-free section ends just after a milepost, arriving on the road by the Cycle Hub **10**. A quiet road section then runs gradually away from the river to join St Lawrence Road. Shortly after heading straight over a mini-roundabout you pass St Peter's Marina down to the right **11**. Pick up the traffic-free path over to your left just here.

KEELMAN'S WAY OPTION
Pass the Baltic **10a** and shortly turn left at a T-junction along South Shore Road, passing through a light industrial area. Where the road turns 90 degrees uphill pick up the path on your left and come to the Kittiwake tower **11a**, especially made for Kittiwakes to nest in after the Baltic centre was renovated.

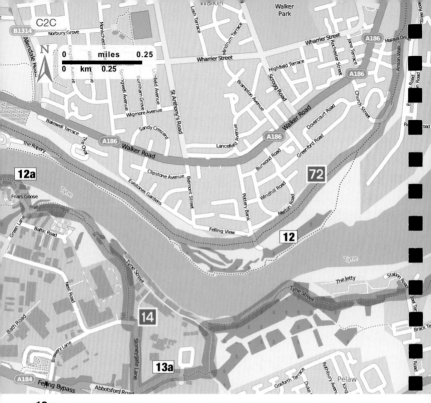

12 The path climbs quickly and gives a great view of St Peter's Marina below you. The next landmark you may see is the riverside cranes of Walker.

KEELMAN'S WAY OPTION
The path runs along the river to Friars Wharf apartments **12a** where it jinks right then left onto another traffic-free section through woods (easy to miss).

Emerge at a road and turn left, bending almost immediately right, uphill. Turn left onto Abbotsford Road **13a**, picking up a traffic-free section again that descends through horse stabling and turns right along the river.

Climb to great views **14a** over the river and the cranes at Walker before dropping down to the river again on a popular parking and fishing spot. Turn left onto the Hebburn Cycleway **15a** before climbing up Ellison Street past a pencil-like church tower **16a** to a T-junction and left on the B1297.

11 CROCKETS HOTEL (PUB)
Mitchell Street Walker
NE6 3PR
0191 2623010 / 07860 671260

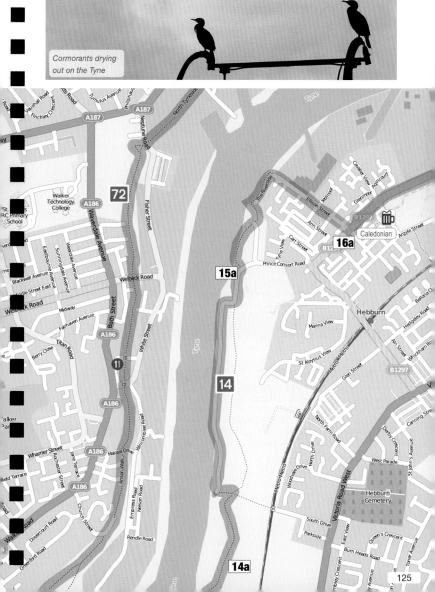

Cormorants drying out on the Tyne

Tyne

A187
A187
Vauxhall Road
Finchley Crescent
Tumulus Avenue
Philiphaugh
Neptune Road
North Tyneside

Walker Technology College
A186
72
St ___ RC Primary School

Waverdale Avenue
Fisher Street

Blackwell Avenue
Eastbourne Avenue
Wearside Avenue
Sunningdale Avenue
Middle Street East
Welbeck Road
Welbeck Road
Midway
Fairhaven Avenue
Bath Street
White Street
A186
Titan Road
Berry Close
11
A186

Walker Park

Wharrier Street
Rochester Street
Jane Terrace
A186
A186
___field Terrace

Empress Road
Nelson Road
Anson Walk
Wincomblee Road
Malaya Drive
Church Street
Rendle Road

Walker Road
Dovercourt Road
Greenford Road

Tyne
Tyne

The Riverside
Ellison Street
Jesmoor
Cavalier View
Agincourt
Glenmoor

Ann Street
Prince Consort Road
Tyne View
Car Street
B12___
Caledonian
16a
B1297
Argyle Street
Betford St

15a

Marina View
Hebburn
Hedgeley Road
Ann Street
Whickham Ro___

14
St Aloysius View
Metro Metro
Glen Street
B1297
V

North Farm Road
Derby Crescent
Canning Stre___
Metro Metro
Woodvale Drive
North Drive
West Parade
St John Street
St Anne's V___
Hebburn Cemetery

South Drive
Parkside
Victoria Road West
East View
Queen's Crescent
Burn Heads Road
___bley Crescent
Toner Avenue
___ Avenue

14a

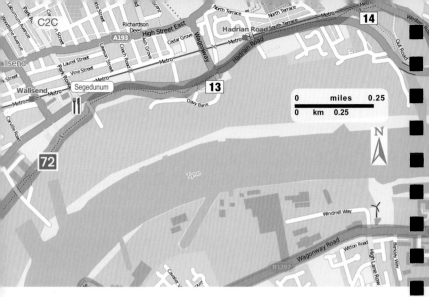

As you pass from Walker into Wallsend you see the viewing tower of Segedunum Roman museum ahead of you. The railpath eventually emerges through a red arch **13** to join pavementside cycle lane past the Hadrian Lodge Hotel.

The cycle lane leaves the pavement and drops down to cross a stream (Willington Gut) **14**. By the spectacular Willington Viaduct you bear right to briefly join Western Road before a short traffic-free section leads to Armstrong Road.

15 Head along Armstrong Road then Auburn Close and across a staggered junction at Howdon Lane **16** to pick up what becomes a traffic-free path. This makes its way across the head of the entrance to the Tyne Tunnel for motor vehicles **17**. A Toucan takes you across a dual carriageway and you join a pavement cycle lane along the south side of the A187.

KEELMAN'S WAY OPTION

It's now simply a matter of following the B1297 all the way to the Tyne pedestrian and cycle tunnel (lifts available) **17a**. Note that it is closed for refurbishment until further notice but there is a replacement bus shuttle service that carries bikes running until the reopening. It operates 6am to 8pm seven days a week.

NCN 14 continues on past the Tyne Tunnel with the option of rejoining the C2C via the ferry from South Shields to North Shields (see page 129 map).

17

A193

Archer Street

Stanley Street

Churchill Street

A193

Howdon
Howdon

Metro

A193

Edwin Grove

Hazelwood Terrace

Firtrees Avenue

Martin Road

Kent Avenue

Howdon Lane

A19

72

16

15

A187

Gulf Road

Western Road

Rosehill Road

Haydon Drive

Armstrong Road

Bewicke Road

A187

A187

Norman Terrace

Bewicke Street

Potter Street

Stephenson Street

A19

Bewicke Street

17a

A187

A19

Tyne Tunnel
New Tyne Tunnel

Howdon Road

Bard Avenue

Northumberland Dock

A19

Tyne

**Tyne pedestrian
& cycle tunnel
(see opposite
for temporary
closure details)**

Tyne Pedestrian Tunnel

A19

Rolling Mill Road

White Lead

B1297

B1297

Witton Road

High Lane Row

Riley Road

Porter Street

14

Martinos

Grange Pl

Chaytor Street

Ferry Street

Ormonde Street

North Street

Water Street

Grange Road

14

Curlew Road

Curlew Road

A19

Saxon Way

Saxon Way

Friar Way

Jarrow

Priory Road

Metro

Metro

Metro

St Oswald's Road

Beech Street

Birch Street

Edith Street

Jarrow

Hill Street

Metro

Metro

Chapel Road

Viking shopping
centre Jarrow

High Street

Staple Road

High Street

Salem Street

Hope Street

St Paul's Road

Albert Road

B1516

York Street

Albert Road

Concorde Way

A185

Metro

A185

Stay on NCN 14 for the Tyne Ferry

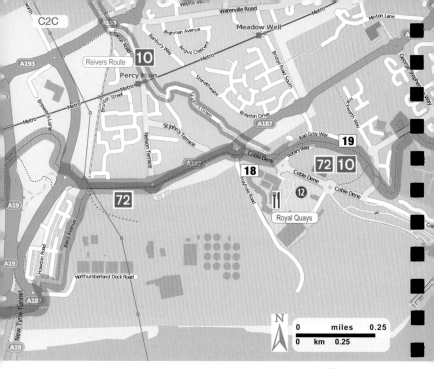

Across two roundabouts you arrive at the Royal Quays shopping centre **18** and a short run along more pavement cycle lane takes you across a toucan to bend right into an attractive landscaped park area, Redburn Dene **19**. Descend past old sea groynes to arrive at a sizeable marina (the ferry terminal to the Netherlands and Scandanavia is at the far side). Bear left to skirt the marina and across the bottom of a series of manmade waterfalls at Chirton Dene.

The road climbs away from the marina on a pavementside cycle track and bears left past the entrance to the Fish Quays **20**. Take the next right (Lawson Street **21**) past light industrial units. At the end of this street jink left then right onto Addison Street.

At the end of Addison Street turn right **22** down Borough Road, under the pedestrian bridge above, and bear left at the bottom by the Porthole pub onto Clive Street, once a den of iniquity, now full of stylish restaurants and bars.

Head past the large brightly painted buoys **23** indicating you are on both NCN routes 72 and 1, and take the wonderful traffic-free path along the north bank of the estuary.

12 PREMIER INN
Coble Dene Road North Shields NE29 6DL
0871 5278820
www.premierinn.com

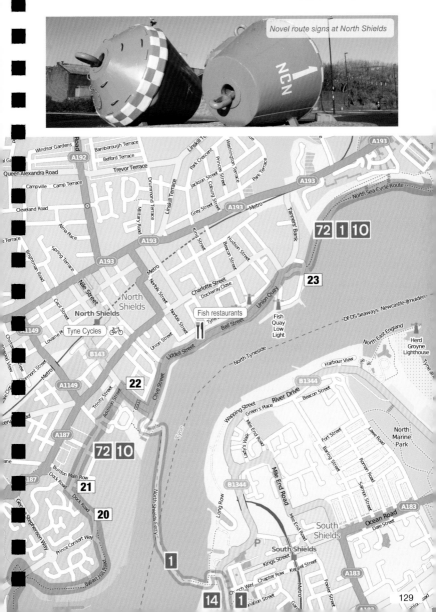

Novel route signs at North Shields

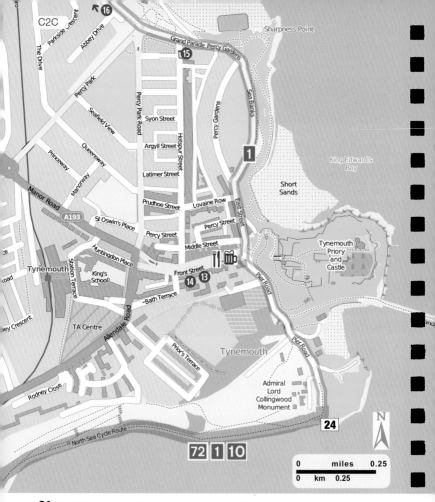

24 The C2C route currently finishes at the end of this stretch of estuaryside riding. However, it is something of an anticlimax and doesn't easily allow for the traditional dipping of the wheel in the sea. If you carry on uphill and onto the front at Tynemouth you will find the magnificent Longsands beach where it's a cinch to wheel your bike onto the beach and drink in the superb views towards Cullercoats and Whitley Bay. The beach is also backed by the stately presence of the Grand Hotel, ideal if you want to splash out on an end of route celebration.

13 MARTINEAU GUEST HOUSE
57 Front Street Tynemouth NE30 4BX
0191 2579038   0793 278 4008
www.martineau-house.co.uk
Weekend min stay requirements

14 SIXTY ONE
61 Front Street Tynemouth NE30 4BT
0191 2573687
www.no61.co.uk

15 THE GRAND HOTEL
Grand Parade Tynemouth NE30 4ER
0191 2936666
www.grandhotel-uk.com

16 MONTAGU PARK HOTEL
Grand Parade Tynemouth NE30 4JQ
0191 2571406
www.parkhoteltynemouth.co.uk

Cyclists approaching Tynemouth
along the Tyne estuary

Appendix I Route Options

The main route options you can choose are detailed below showing how much distance and height they add (or if preceded by a - sign this means they save distance or climbing height). So you can see at a glance that the only true shortcut is the unsigned route along the valley bottom avoiding Mungrisdale. By contrast the Stanhope alternative adds the most in terms of distance and climbing.

Route	From	To	Distance & height added or saved (-)
Castlerigg Stone Circle & the Old Coach Road	Keswick railpath	Greystoke	1.6km / 1mi 174m / 571ft
Alston alternative	Leadgate	Alston	0.6km / 0.4mi -134m / 442ft
Valley bottom avoiding Mungrisdale (unsigned)	Scales	West of Troutbeck	-5km / 3.2mi -118m / 380ft
Garrigill off-road	Garrigill	Nenthead	3.2km / 2 mi 22m / 75ft
Stanhope alternative	Rookhope	Waskerley Way (Parkhead)	3.2km / 2mi 184m / 604ft
Keelman's Way (south bank of the Tyne)	Near confluence of Derwent & Tyne rivers	Tyne Tunnel	1.6km / 1mi 54m / 179ft

Appendix II Linking Routes

National Cycle Network also provides handy link routes between the start points and end points of the C2C which may prove useful, depending on the logistics of your arrival and departure, or if you just wish to see a bit more of the area.

Route	From	To	Length / height climbed
Hadrian's Cycleway / Reivers	Whitehaven	Workington	14km / 8.7mi 240m / 788ft
Three Rivers	South Shields (via ferry from North Shields)	Sunderland	15.5km / 9.6mi 234m / 768ft

National Cycle Network

C2C FINISH

START

Hadrian's Cycleway

Reivers

Coast & Castles

1

Want to extend your journey on the National Cycle Network? Tynemouth is the hub of a variety of other signed cycle routes. NCN mapping for all of the UK is at:

www.sustrans.org.uk

Where ❯
❮ will you go
next? ❯

Check out more long-distance routes available from Sustrans

Pennine Cycleway North
Cycle Route Map

Pennine Cycleway South
Cycle Route Map

Land's End to John o'Groats
on the National Cycle Network

South Coast East
Cycle Route Map

South Coast West
Cycle Route Map

shop.sustrans.org.uk

sustrans

Greystoke Cycle Café Tea Garden

is a lovely walled tea garden near Greystoke Castle, directly on the C2C & E2E routes just 5 miles from Penrith, J40 of the M6 and the northern Lakes. Gazebos & barns provide shelter. We open seasonally during June July & August, (please check website for full details) and then are open to cyclists on bikes every day 10-6pm (groups please pre book). We're open to those arriving on foot (we have

no parking as such) on Friday 12-6pm Sat 10-6pm & 2nd Sun of the month 10-6pm, please enjoy the 300yd stroll from the village, often alongside racehorses. Our limited parking is reserved for cycle support.

See www.greystokecyclecafe.co.uk   017684 80613

Guardian 'Top UK Tea & Cakes Stops' ~ Top 10 Cyclists Cafés in Cycling Weekly & Cycling Plus.

Quirky Workshops

Take place at the Cycle Café throughout the year; many who discover us on their journey return later to try a workshop in Greystoke. Offering an unrivalled range of courses since 2005 in bike maintenance, longbow making, wood sculpture/ whittling. engraving, calligraphy, mosaics, leatherwork, furniture and upholstery, pole lathe, blacksmithing/knife forging, 'hands on' artisan baking & cheesemaking, garden sculptures in willow or wire, dowsing, printing, silver jewellery, fused or stained glass, stone carving, textiles including felt, rag rug, loom weaving, pattern cutting, spinning, crochet and needlefelt – and lots more. New from 2018 is lime plastering.

www.quirkyworkshops.co.uk   017684 83984

Dowsing & Divining

Helios

Morpheus

You can
also hire
our bikes

www.circecycles.com
+44 (0)1954 782020

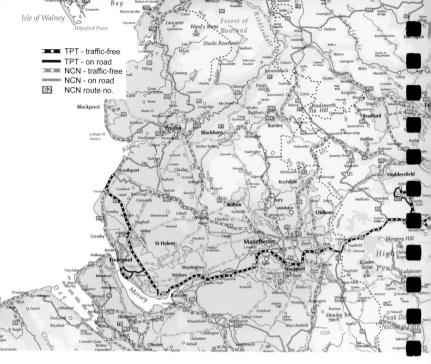

Why not try the Trans Pennine Trail?

- The Uk's first long-distance multi-user trail with 350 miles of tracks, trails and minor roads available to walkers and cyclists with many sections available to horseriders and wheelchair users too

- The ideal family trail for either a long distance coast to coast adventure or a day out

- Around two-thirds traffic-free using railpaths, canal towpaths and woodland tracks

- Countless family and visitor attractions en-route

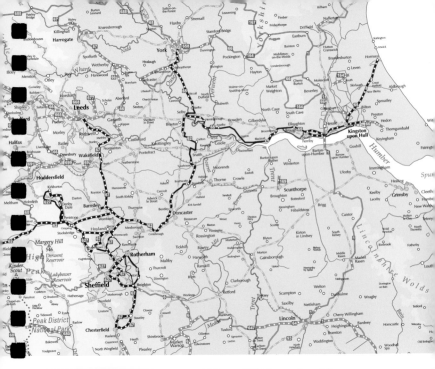

The Ultimate Trans Pennine Trail Guide

The Ultimate Trans Pennine Trail Guide

* Detailed full colour 1:75,000 mapping showing route options for cyclists, walkers and horse-riders.

* Street-level mapping for main towns including: Southport, Liverpool, Widnes, Stockport, Penistone, Doncaster, Chesterfield, Sheffield, Leeds, Selby, Hull and Hornsea.
* Numerous colour images.

Available at www.excellentbooks.co.uk

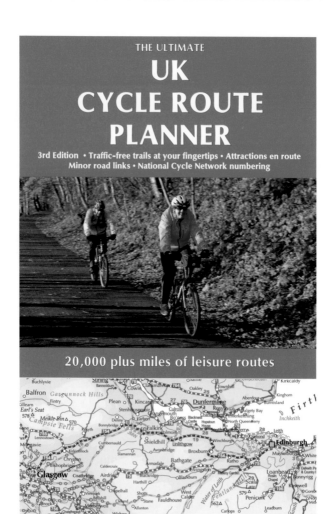

The Ultimate UK Cycle Route Planner

3rd Edition · Traffic-free trails at your fingertips · Attractions en route
Minor road links · National Cycle Network numbering

20,000 plus miles of leisure routes

New updated printing out now

* All UK signed cycle routes on one map * Sustrans National Cycle Network
route numbering * Attractions (stately homes, country parks, museums etc)
* Rail access * And lots more!

Interchangeable monkii System

monkii cage

Clip it on. Clip it off

Carry a bottle / Thermos
from 0.5L to 1.5L

Tough construction

Flexible to carry narrow or
wide containers

Won't scratch your bottle

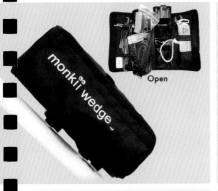

monkii V wedge

Clip it on. Clip it off

For your tools and
repair essentials

Tough construction

Fill it. Roll it
(strong hook & loop closure)

*Tools shown for display purposes only

monkii mono

Clip it on. Clip it off

For your essential items
and valuables

Tough water resistant
construction

Twin zips for easy access